Genesis One and the Origin of the Earth

Robert C. Newman
Herman J. Eckelmann, Jr.

BAKER BOOK HOUSE
Grand Rapids, Michigan 49506

Reprinted 1981 by Baker Book House Company
ISBN: 0-8010-6735-9

Printed in the United States of America

To Ian Axford, Frank Drake, Thomas Gold, Martin Harwit and Carl Sagan

Acknowledgments

Since the present book is a proposal rather than a survey, no attempt has been made to note more than a small fraction of the voluminous literature which has been published on this subject. Instead, a few works which are easily obtainable have been cited to indicate a particular viewpoint or to note a datum of science or of the biblical text. Because this work is written to be read by some who know science but not exegesis, and vice versa, technical words and terminology from both fields have been avoided as much as possible.

Special acknowledgment is due to Herman J. Eckelmann, Jr., who, though not responsible for the final form of this work, has been so instrumental in certain aspects of the model proposed that any recognition less than co-authorship would be unfair. For valuable discussions I thank Prof. Robert J. Dunzweiler, Dr. Perry G. Phillips and Dr. Robert W. Manweiler. My thanks also to Daniel E. Wonderly and R. John Snow for permission to include their papers as appendices of this work.

Most of all I thank the Lord God Almighty, Maker of heaven and earth, and Jesus Christ, his only Son. May this work be used to magnify God's name in the hearts of men.

Contents

Part II Theology

Illustrations

Figure

Tables

About the Contributors

Robert C. Newman is a graduate of Duke University (B.S., physics), Cornell University (Ph.D., astrophysics), Faith Theological Seminary (M.Div.) and Biblical Theological Seminary (S.T.M., Old Testament), and he has taken graduate work in religious thought at the University of Pennsylvania. He was formerly a Post-Doctoral Fellow with the Bartol Research Foundation of the Franklin Institute and Associate Professor of Physics and Mathematics at Shelton College. He is presently Professor of New Testament at Biblical Theological Seminary, where he teaches courses in apologetics and the interaction of science and Christianity. Dr. Newman has written articles for scientific and theological journals, and he is co-author with Peter W. Stoner of *Science Speaks.* He is a fellow of the Interdisciplinary Biblical Research Institute and the American Astronomical Society and the Evangelical Theological Society.

R. John Snow is a graduate of King's College (B.S., mathematics), Bowling Green State University (M.A., mathematics) and Grace Theological Seminary (M.Div.). He taught mathematics on the secondary school level for seven years in Ithaca, N.Y. Entering the ministry in 1974, he has served in Grace Brethren Churches in Elizabethtown and Johnstown, Pa. He is presently pastor of the Grace Brethren Church of Orleans, Vt.

Herman J. Eckelmann, Jr., (B.S.E.E., Cornell University; M.Div., Faith Theological Seminary) is pastor of the Faith Bible Church of Ithaca, N.Y. He was a research associate with the Center for Radiophysics and Space Research at Cornell University, and has been instrumental in the conversion or turning to specifically Christian work of a number of students there and at Ithaca College. Pastor Eckelmann is on the Board of Trustees of Biblical Theological Seminary, an associate of the Interdisciplinary Biblical Research Institute, a member of the American Scientific Affiliation, and a popular lecturer on Christian evidences.

William Henry Green (1825-1900), a graduate of Lafayette College and Princeton Theological Seminary, spent his entire teaching career at the latter institution, where he was Professor of Oriental and Old Testament Literature from 1859 until his death. Professor Green was President of the Faculty for seventeen years, declined an offer to be President of the College of New Jersey (later Princeton University), and served as chairman of the Old Testament section of the American Bible Revision Committee. He wrote a number of books, including *Grammar of the Hebrew Language* (1861), *The Hebrew Feasts* (1885), *General Introduction to the Old Testament* (1898), as well as several works responding to critical theories regarding the origin of the Pentateuch.

Daniel E. Wonderly is a graduate of Wheaton College (A.B., anthropology), Central Baptist Seminary (B.D., Th.M.) and Ohio University (M.S., biological science). He has done graduate work at various universities in embryology, paleontology and several areas of geology, including studies of sedimentology in Bermuda. Professor Wonderly has taught Bible and anthropology at Southeastern Bible College (1952-55), zoology at Wingate Junior College (1961-66), and several areas of biology at Grace College (1966-73). He is a member of a number of scientific societies, the author of *God's Time-Records in Ancient Sediments* (1977), and is presently engaged in research and writing in the area of geology and the Bible.

Introduction

Modern science, in alliance with technology since the seventeenth century, has revolutionized our knowledge of the world and transformed the material aspects of everyday life. Whereas men once saw the earth as the physical center of the universe, around which the sun, moon, stars and planets moved in a complex dance, it is now apparent that our home is a small satellite of an average star which is only one member of a large galaxy in a vast but unfathomed universe. Only two centuries ago the fastest modes of travel were the horse and the sailing ship, and a hundred miles' journey was a major feat for one day. Today, thousands cross an ocean or a continent in a matter of hours, and astronauts circle the globe in an hour or travel to the moon and back in a week.

Many now claim that, along with archaic concepts and antique transportation, God too is a remnant of man's ignorance and prescientific superstitions. In spite of good evidence that Christianity played a significant part in the rise of modern science and in its union with once-despised technology,[1] some argue that "since man originally made God to explain the mysteries of nature, he can now dispense with Him." In seeking to prove that God is merely an invention of ancient (or medieval) man, the Philosophe movement of eighteenth-century France first began to allege contradictions between science and Christianity.[2] This line of attack has been continued to the present, with the result that many have rejected Christianity in favor of science, while others have spurned science to cling to Christianity.

The area of origins is one of the principal points where such contradiction has been alleged. Science is said to show us an eternal universe which naturally produced the earth and then life upon it billions of years ago, culminating (so far) in the evolution of man a few million years ago from the higher forms of animal life. To the extent that it is consistent with the Bible, Christianity, by contrast, is thought to teach that only God is eternal and that he miraculously created the earth and everything on it in six literal, consecutive days only a few thousand years ago.

Many people accept this characterization as a clear demonstration of the conflict between science and the Bible, if not between science and Christianity. But an unambiguous case for this conflict is still lacking. Ideally, science seeks a true description of the physical world through study of the observable data of nature. Christianity seeks a true description of the spiritual world through study of the revealed data of Scripture. Neither of these descriptions is obtained by popular vote. Instead, researchers in each field construct models (or hypotheses) which, in competition with other models, must run the gauntlet of critical scrutiny and argument.

Among those who consider the Bible an authoritative revelation from God, this strong tension over origins has resulted in the appearance of a wide spectrum of views regarding the relationship between science and the Bible. At one end of this spectrum are certain theistic evolutionists who accept whatever consensus on origins there is among scientists, adding only that the God revealed in the Bible is behind it all.[3] At the other end are some proponents of recent creationism who continue to maintain Archbishop Ussher's date of 4004 B.C. for the creation. In order to rule out any data which seem to point to an older earth or universe, they are ready to make extensive use of the idea that God created with the appearance of age.[4]

The authors of this work consider the Bible to be the authoritative, inerrant revelation of God. It does not follow from this, however, that (1) the scientific models regarding the age of the earth and the universe must be overthrown in order to maintain the scientific authority of Scripture, or that (2) the scientific authority of Scripture must be reduced to a few propositions like "God is behind it all." Although neither theistic evolution nor recent creationism is necessarily as extreme as the ends of the spectrum above indicate, our position is to be identified with neither of these. We advocate a third, intermediate view usually labeled "progressive creationism."[5]

Our discussion is limited to a single facet of origins—the physical origin of the planet Earth. Attention is first directed to the physical data which appear to be relevant to a scientific model of the origin of the earth. Next, from among the serious options, a model for the synthesis of the scientific and biblical data is selected and defended on scientific grounds. We then will consider the biblical data, noting especially the points at which the traditional interpretation is or is not required by the Hebrew text. Accordingly, modifications of the traditional understanding are suggested which allow a synthesis of the scientific and biblical data into a "unified field" theory of the origin of the earth.

This proposal is based on the assumption that the data of Scripture and the data of science are both true, but that the simplest possible interpretation of either set of data taken alone will not necessarily give the complete picture, nor even a correct picture. Thus the question of origins according to the scientific and scriptural data is analogous to the problem of the chronology of the kings of Israel and Judah according to the archaeological and biblical data, which was solved very nicely by Thiele on the assumption that both sets of data were valid if properly interpreted.[6]

This model provides a correlation between science and Scripture in place of the contradiction commonly imagined. If valid, this correlation could have far-reaching implications both for the general reliability of the scientific method for investigation of prehistory, and for the scientific reliability and divine inspiration of Scripture.

Part I
Science

1

Chronological Evidence from Scientific Data

The question of the age of man, the earth and the universe is one of the principal points of disagreement between science and the Bible as commonly understood. Therefore, our discussion of the scientific data begins with chronology. The chronological data in the Bible is discussed in chapter 4.

As the age of man is not directly relevant to our restricted study, we shall be looking only at the scientific data concerning the age of the earth and the universe. This material may be classed under two headings: astronomical evidence and geological evidence.

Astronomical Evidence: Light Travel-Time

There are several types of astronomical data which give us estimates for the age of the universe, the sun and the solar system (which includes the earth). Each estimate is based upon somewhat different assumptions, and gives ages for distinct events.

Light is the name we give to the visible portion of the spectrum of electromagnetic radiation. It has wavelengths from about 0.4 micron to 0.7 micron, or roughly 2 millionths of a foot. Observations made on earth indicate that light travels at a constant speed of about 186,000 miles per second in a vacuum, but somewhat slower in a material medium. Thus light takes about 8½ minutes to reach the earth from the sun, about 6 hours from the planet Pluto, and about 4 years from the nearest star.

Therefore a minimum estimate of the age of the universe can be made, subject to the following assumptions: (1) light has traveled at this speed everywhere in space throughout the history of the universe; (2) the light we observe actually came from the stars and other astronomical objects that it pictures; and (3) our distance measurements for these objects are sufficiently accurate. According to this argument, then, the universe is at least as old as the light travel-time calculated for the most distant astronomical objects we have observed.

Concerning the third assumption, it must be admitted that the measurement of astronomical distances is a complicated matter. Nevertheless, increasing accuracy is being obtained by improved instruments and by the multiplication of methods which serve as a cross-check upon one another.[1] The distances to the nearest stars are measured directly by observing their apparent shift with respect to the distant stars as the earth travels around the sun. This "parallax" method is good out to about 600 trillion miles (100 light-years), in which range there are about ten thousand stars. This direct method requires only that the universe be older than one hundred years.

These ten thousand stars have been carefully studied, and a simple relationship between the color and the actual brightness of a certain class of these stars (the so-called "main sequence" stars) has been determined. This allows astronomers to compare observed brightness with actual brightness in large star clusters and thereby to measure their distances accurately out to about 300,000 light-years. Already, with this second method, it is clear that if assumptions (1) and (2) hold, the universe is much older than a few thousand years.

Billions of stars are now within the range of our distance measurements. Studies have been made on rarer objects among this group, such as certain types of stars which fluctuate periodically in brightness. Some of these are known as Cepheid variable stars. The greater their actual brightness is, the longer they take to complete their cycle from dim to bright and back. Another group, called RR Lyrae stars, all have about the same actual brightness. Knowing the apparent brightness of such stars as seen from the earth, we can calculate then how far away they are. The Cepheid variable and RR Lyrae stars are bright enough to be seen 50 times farther away than the group whose distances were determined by main sequence stars, so that we can now measure distances beyond 10 million light-years. This brings within range the nearby galaxies. If assumptions (1) and (2) are correct, then the universe is at least 10 million years old.

Observation of astronomical objects within this vastly expanded volume indicates that there is a maximum brightness among stars, among certain clusters of stars, and even among galaxies. If we then observe the apparent brightness of the brightest stars in more distant clusters or galaxies, the apparent brightness of the brightest globular clusters in distant galaxies, or the brightest galaxy in a cluster of galaxies, we may calculate their distances from the fact that the brightness of an object appears to decrease inversely with the square of the distance. This method is good out to the limit of visibility of stars and globular clusters (about 100 million light-years), or to the limit of visibility of galaxies (several billion light-years). Thus the universe would be at least several billion years old.

The most distant astronomical objects known appear to be the so-called quasars. These are so far away as to look like mere points of light in the largest telescopes, yet radiate energy far in excess of the largest known galaxies. If the frequency-shift of the radiation emitted by quasars is due entirely to the expansion of our universe (see discussion p. 20) then the most distant known quasars are over 10 billion light-years away. Consequently, the universe is more than 10 billion years old.[2]

But is it possible that assumptions (1) and (2) are incorrect? There is, of course, no way for man to *prove* that the speed of light is a constant throughout the universe and throughout history. Still, by assuming the constancy of the speed of light, astronomers can understand and accurately predict many things about other stars from the study of our sun and from various experiments in earthbound laboratories. This fact suggests that assumption (1) is reasonable. To my knowledge, however, no proponents of a young earth have denied assumption (1).

On the other hand, it is common among those who think the earth is only a few thousand years old to deny assumption (2), asserting that the light we observe from distant stars never really left such stars, but was created *en route* and has only been traveling for a few thousand years.[3] To the objection that this scheme implies God is giving man a misleading impression about the age of the earth, young-earth advocates say that God gives the true age in the Bible. We shall examine their exegesis in chapter 4. It is sufficient to note here two further problems. First, since light travels at a finite speed, the light we see from an astronomical object (with all its information on the composition, luminosity, rotation and motion of the object) tells us what the object was doing when the light left it. Thus light from the sun indicates what was happening there 8½ minutes earlier; from Pluto, 6 hours earlier; from the nearest star, 4 years earlier. But does light from, say, the Andromeda galaxy (about 2 million light-years away) tell us what the galaxy would have been doing if it had been created 2 million years ago, though it was actually created only ten thousand years ago? Second, if astronomical observation gives a misleading impression about age, it equally well may give a mistaken idea about distance and even about the number of stars, since the light we observe never left the stars it pictures. Following this methodology, it is difficult to avoid complete scepticism, for one could claim that the whole universe (including our memories) was created two seconds ago.

A rather ingenious suggestion has been proposed recently which seeks to avoid the evidence of light travel-time for an old universe without falling into the problem of having light created *en route* from distant stars. This hypothesis, as described by Harold S. Slusher,[4] claims that light follows a different path through space than a planet or space ship would; namely, that for light, the universe is curved with a radius of about five light-years. As a result, light from the most distant stars reached earth within twenty years of creation (pi x 5 years), and consequently we can see the most distant reaches of space today. Slusher's discussion is based on an article in the *Journal of the Optical Society of America*,[5] which suggests that by this stratagem the evidence of certain binary stars in favor of Einstein's special theory of relativity may be avoided.

But when one stops to think what the universe must look like according to this curved light-space theory, no reasonable image appears: If the paths of all light rays in the universe have a curvature of five light-years, then it would be impossible to see any object more than ten light-years away (twice the radius of curvature). The effect would be similar to standing between two parallel mirrors in a clothing store. In the mirrors you see hundreds of images of yourself dwindling off to infinity. At first we might suppose that this is what the universe looks like—many repeated images of a few stars. But there are only about a hundred stars within ten light-years. Are we to believe that a hundred stars, even multiplied many times by reflection, yield a picture looking like the Milky Way? or the Andromeda galaxy? or the various galaxy clusters? A few minutes' examination of astronomical photographs should convince one of the absurdity of this suggestion.

Astronomical Evidence: Expansion of the Universe

Another line of evidence for the age of the universe involves the apparent recession of the galaxies. In the 1920s Edwin Hubble extended the earlier work of V. M. Slipher by turning the newly-built 100-inch reflecting telescope at Mt. Wilson Observatory toward the galaxies. He confirmed Slipher's observation that their light was red-shifted. That is, spectroscopic lines appeared at longer wavelengths when observed in the light from galaxies than when observed in light produced in an earthbound laboratory. Hubble also noticed that this effect was progressive: more distant galaxies showed a greater red-shift.[6]

The simplest explanation for such a red-shift would be the movement of the galaxies away from us and from each other. In other words, the universe is expanding. This shift, called the Doppler effect, is similar to the apparent lowering of the pitch of an auto horn or train whistle when the vehicle is moving away from you.

Other explanations, such as reddening due to the gravitational pull of the source or of objects passed on the way, or reddening due to scattering from dust along the way, will not fit the observations. The suggestion that light gets "tired" as it travels is possible, but depends on the assumption of an otherwise unknown physical law. Therefore this view has not been widely accepted.

But if the universe is understood to be expanding, extrapolation backward in time would cram all of the galaxies into a relatively small volume at some time in the past. Old-earth creationists see this time as the date of creation, although most astrophysicists, anxious to avoid supernatural intervention, prefer to see this "pile-up" as the result of a previous contraction.[7]

At present, the most accurate figure available for the expansion of the universe is 55 ± 7 kilometers per second per Megaparsec, which would give the elapsed time since the maximum compression or creation as 17.7 ± 3 billion years.[8] This, then, is another estimate for the age of the universe, consistent with the previous estimate based on light travel-time, but dependent on a different set of assumptions: (1) distances to galaxies can be measured with reasonable accuracy; (2) the measured red-shift is due to expansion; and (3) the universe is as old as this maximum compression (the so-called big bang).

Assumption (1) was discussed in the previous section. Assumption (2) cannot be proved, but it is the only hypothesis using known laws which fits the data. The third assumption is open to question in two directions. First, proponents of the cosmologies known as the *steady-state theory* and the *oscillating big-bang theory* assume the universe is infinitely old. Each must postulate new and unknown physical laws to get around the fact that the simple extrapolation of known laws leads back to a mathematical singularity (the density of matter becomes infinite) at the time of the *big bang.*[9]

On the other hand, proponents of a young earth claim that the expansion never started from the big bang, but rather from some more expanded configuration only a few thousand years ago. Radiotelescopes, however, observe a uniform background of radiation; that is, to a radiotelescope the sky looks gray rather than black, as it looks through an optical telescope. This is naturally explained by "big bang theories" (oscillating or not) as the remnant of the early hot period in the expansion of the universe some 17.7 billion years ago.[10] Both the steady-state and young-earth views must resort to ad hoc explanations for this radiation.

Here again, as in the case of light travel-time, the simplest explanation of the astronomical data suggests a universe more than 10 billion years old. In addition, this method gives a more specific age in the range of 15 billion to 20 billion years.

Astronomical Evidence: Stellar Structure

So far, our considerations of age based on astronomical data have involved very simple calculations in which the major factor was the movement of light or of galaxies through space. Now, however, we must turn to much more complex calculations involving the details of the insides of stars.

Though far simpler in structure than planets, stars are still quite complex. A star is an enormous quantity of very hot gas held together by its own gravity. The gravitational contraction is resisted by thermal pressure, which is itself strongly dependent on heat sources within the star. Calculations are complicated by the fact that stars contain small quantities of elements heavier than their main constituents (hydrogen and helium). Further, the structure of the star will vary drastically depending on what nuclear processes are occurring in its core, whether the heat is carried to the surface by radiation or convection, the degree of opacity of various layers within the star, and whether stellar rotation and magnetism are significant.[11]

Nevertheless, the development of electronic computers since World War 2 has made possible detailed calculations for the interior structure of stars under a wide variety of circumstances. Calculations have also included attempts to trace the life cycle of a star from its birth as a gas cloud through its various stages to its death as a white dwarf, a neutron star or a black hole. An outline of these various stages is pertinent.[12]

First is the contraction phase. A gas cloud gradually contracts from a size of perhaps one light-year across with a very low temperature (perhaps a hundred degrees absolute) to sun-size (a few hundred thousand miles in diameter) with temperatures of several thousand degrees at the surface and several million degrees inside. During this phase, the main heat source of the star is the gravitational energy derived from the contraction itself. This phase lasts some millions of years.

But as the temperature reaches about 10 million degrees Kelvin at the center of the star, a nuclear reaction transmuting hydrogen into helium begins which is similar to that in a hydrogen bomb. This reaction is a powerful source of heat, and quickly builds up enough pressure to stop the gravitational contraction as long as hydrogen "fuel" is available in the core to sustain the reaction. The star thus enters its so-called main sequence phase. At the rate our sun burns its fuel, its hydrogen should last about 10 billion years. The stronger gravity of a star much larger than the sun increases the interior temperature, thus causing the hydrogen fuel to be consumed in as little as a million years. Much smaller stars would stay on the main sequence up to a trillion years.

When the hydrogen in the core of the star has been exhausted, the core again begins to contract under the force of gravity. This contraction heats up the interior and causes the outer part of the star to expand. As a result, the star becomes much larger (though less dense), but also cooler at its surface. This is the *red giant* phase. When the core temperature rises to about 100 million degrees, the helium in the core begins to transmute into carbon by a new nuclear reaction. This reaction produces less energy per unit mass of fuel than did the hydrogen-helium fusion, so the red giant stage does not last as long as the main sequence phase—a few hundred million years for a star the size of the sun. A brief period in which the carbon is converted to heavier elements follows, and then the star begins to "die."

The death of a star may be violent or relatively quiet, depending on its mass. Some stars will pass through periods in which they fluctuate in brightness; some will explode violently. Whatever remains when the stellar fuel is exhausted will resume its gravitational collapse. Stars which at this point have masses no larger than 1.2 times that of the present sun will gradually contract into *white dwarf* stars, consisting of a mass of electrons and protons weighing several tons per cubic inch. Thereafter, in the course of trillions of years, the star will slowly cool off, cease to radiate, and become a *black dwarf*.

It is thought that stars heavier than 1.2 times the mass of the sun become *neutron stars* instead of white dwarfs. The electrons and protons combine to form neutrons which take up much less space than the normal nuclear structure. The resulting star would be less than 20 miles in diameter and would weigh millions of tons per cubic inch! Still heavier stars are thought to continue beyond the neutron star phase to become *black holes*, in which the space itself is bent to form a kind of closed bag from which not even light can escape!

By now you may be wondering, "What does all this have to do with chronology?" Actually, a great deal. Here is a theoretical explanation for the life cycle of stars which shows a rather detailed fit with the observed properties of stars. If the surface temperature and actual brightness of the several thousand stars for which we can measure distances by the parallax method are graphed, the result is called a Hertzsprung-Russell diagram (figure 1). These stars, chosen for nearness to the sun, are scattered over most of the diagram (though with very thick concentrations along the main sequence line, and in the red giant and white dwarf areas) and therefore seem to have a wide range of ages.

If, however, instead of the nearby stars, we graph only the stars in a given star cluster, a much less scattered diagram results (figure 2). By comparing diagrams from var-

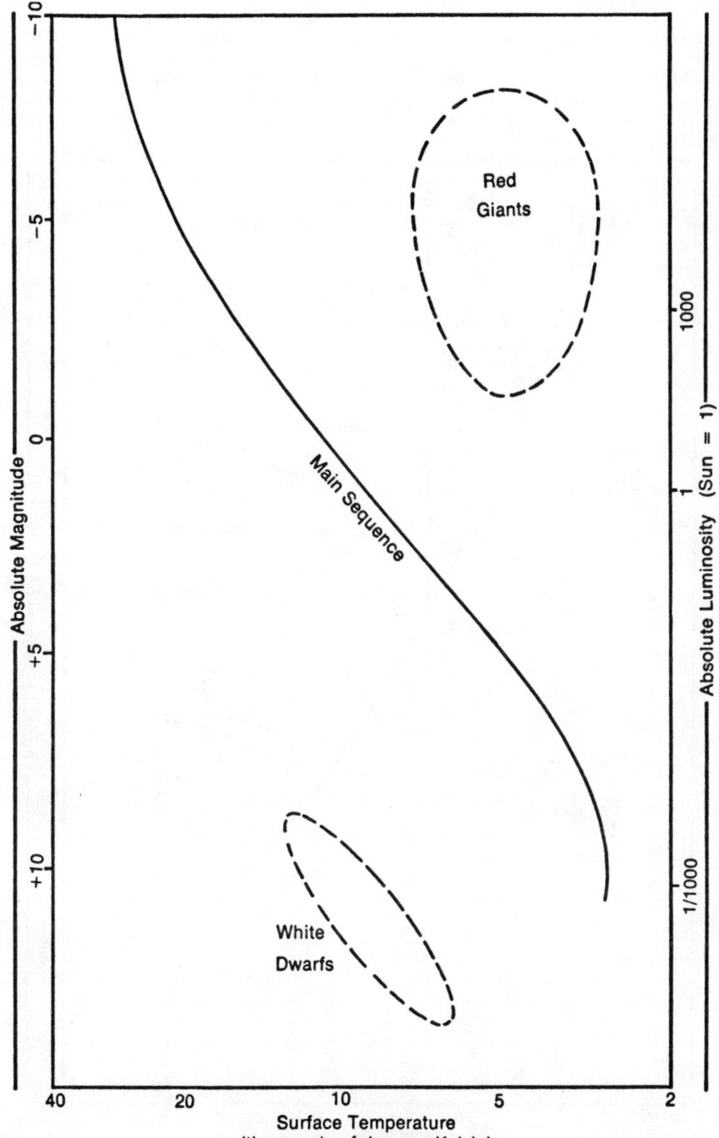

Figure 1: Sketch of the Distribution of Nearby and Brightest Stars. The absolute magnitude of a star is defined as the apparent brightness it would have if it were a standard distance away (10 parsecs, or about 32.6 light-years). Adapted from Robert Jastrow and Malcolm H. Thompson, *Astronomy: Fundamentals and Frontiers*, 2nd ed. (New York: John Wiley and Sons, 1974), p. 129.

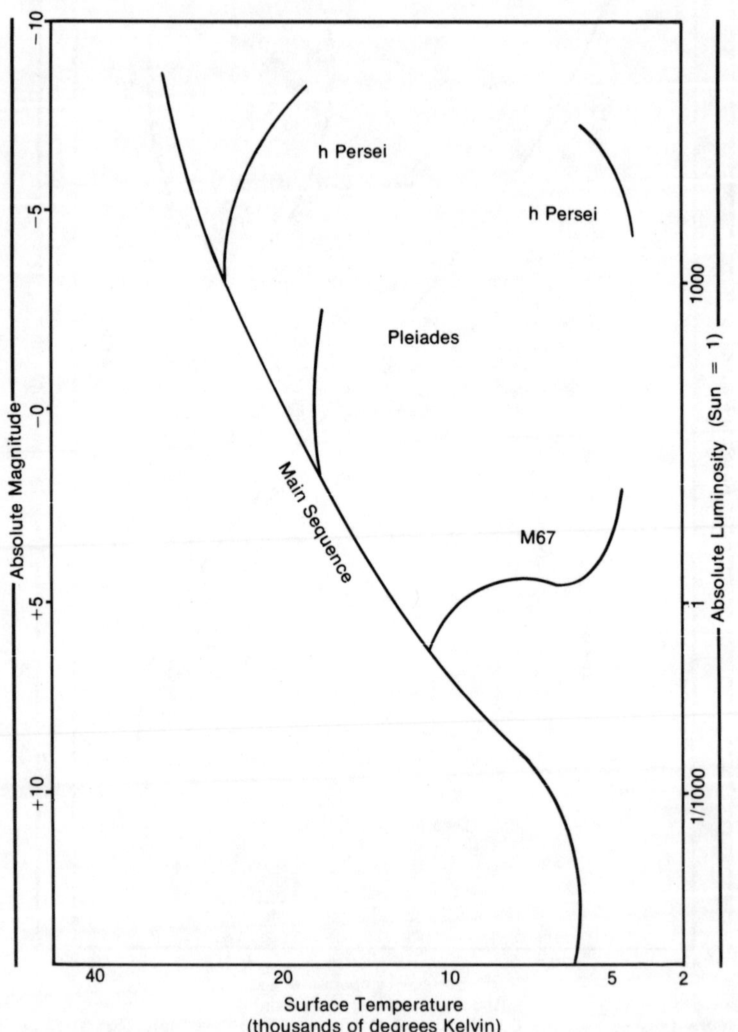

Figure 2: Sketch of Several Star Clusters Compared with the Zero-Age Main Sequence. Adapted from George Abell, *Exploration of the Universe*, 3rd ed. (New York: Holt, Rinehart and Winston, 1975), p. 563.

ious star clusters with stellar theory, we find that the individual stars in a cluster usually have about the same age, but that the ages of the clusters vary widely. In the Hertzsprung-Russell diagram, this shows up most clearly in the heavier stars which, being more luminous, burn their hydrogen more rapidly and move away from the main sequence into the red giant region.

Thus stars in a cluster which have just begun to burn their hydrogen into helium will lie totally along the main sequence. Neglecting the time necessary for the stars of the cluster to form by contraction from gas clouds, such a cluster would have an age of zero. In fact, we call the line described by stars of various masses which have just begun to burn their hydrogen the "zero-age" main sequence. For older clusters, the Hertzsprung-Russell diagram shows their stars departing from the zero-age main sequence at some minimum magnitude (maximum brightness), varying with age, because the larger stars have already moved into the red giant region (phase).

In the cluster h Persei, for example, the brightest star remaining on the main sequence has an absolute magnitude of about −4 and the cluster by comparison with computer calculations of the development of stars would be only about 10 million years old. The corresponding star distribution for the Pleiades leaves the main sequence at zero magnitude and is nearly 100 million years old. The cluster M67 departs from the main sequence at magnitude +4 and is about 4 billion years old.[13]

From this chronological technique it appears that stars have been forming over the whole history of the universe, from 15 billion to 20 billion years ago until today,[14] and that our own Milky Way galaxy is about as old as the universe. Our sun appears to be substantially younger than our galaxy—only 5 to 10 billion years old.[15] Some of the oldest star clusters in our galaxy have a composition different from our sun and the younger star clusters in that they contain very little of the heavier elements. It thus appears that the heavy elements, formed in the interior of *first generation* stars, were then scattered by explosions and became part of the younger stars such as our sun.[16]

This chronological method depends on several assumptions: (1) the observed physical laws hold throughout (at least) the nearby universe over its entire history; (2) our understanding of these laws is adequate for these calculations; and (3) the stars were not created instantaneously somewhere in the midst of their life cycles. The first of these is basically a uniformity principle and, though it cannot be proved, seems to be consistent with the vast majority of observations. Opponents of this principle, in order to get a hearing in scientific circles, are obligated to propose an alternative postulate which demonstrably explains a comparable amount of data.

The second assumption is also difficult to test. The sun, the only star we are reasonably close to, is an average star in an average part of its life cycle (main sequence). Much work can be done in laboratories on earth or in nuclear explosions which is relevant to the behavior of stars, but it is not possible to match all the physical conditions in this way. A great deal depends on the mathematical simulation of stellar conditions by electronic computers. Of course, billions of stars are carefully watched by astronomers. These provide both input data and a check on theoretical models.

The third assumption, likewise, cannot be checked directly. Those who believe that the Genesis account requires a universe only a few thousand years old will naturally assume that the stars were created instantaneously at various stages in their life cycles. This resurrects the problem of "creation with apparent age" mentioned earlier. We shall discuss this further in connection with biblical evidence regarding chronology. At this point we merely note that in the light of evidence that star formation is going on even now,[17] it appears that not all stars were formed at some moment of creation a few thousand years ago.

Meteorites and Lunar Material

Another source of astronomical age information is actual material from outer space. The fall of minerals from the sky has been recognized in scientific circles for about two centuries. Dating this material has been undertaken in this century since the development of geological dating methods. Since the United States landed men on the moon in 1969, minerals from the lunar surface and immediate subsurface have also been available for study.

Because the methods and assumptions used in dating extraterrestrial matter are similar to those used for geological materials, we shall reserve our discussion of these for the next section. Here let us note that meteoritic materials show ages for their most recent crystallization which range upward to 4.5 billion years, which is thought to be the date of the formation of the solar system.[18] Most lunar rocks so far examined are younger—about 3.5 billion years old—though one sample seems to be about 4.5 billion years old.[19] The moon appears to have formed with the rest of the solar system, but also to have experienced extensive surface melting a billion years later.

Summary of Astronomical Evidence

We have discussed three methods for gathering and interpreting astronomical evidences of age. Each method depends on somewhat different assumptions, and each gives ages for different events. The first, the light travel-time method, suggests that the universe is older than the time necessary for light to reach us from the most distant known astronomical object. With our present knowledge, this object is a quasar and the time is about 10 billion years.

Secondly, the apparent expansion of the universe is observed in the red-shifted spectra of galaxies. This observation together with a uniform radio-wavelength radiation, which seems to be the remnant of the "big bang" fireball, suggests that the universe was created a finite time in the past in a very compact condition. The best measurements of these red-shifts and the distances of galaxies indicate that this compacted condition existed 15 billion to 20 billion years ago.

Studies of the structure and energy sources of stars enable us to compute the ages of individual stars and, with even greater accuracy, star clusters. This third method gives an age of the universe consistent with the above methods: our galaxy is the same age as, or slightly younger than, the universe, and the sun—5 billion to 10 billion years old—is substantially younger than the universe or our galaxy. (Mineralogical methods give ages of about 4.5 billion years for the formation of the moon and the meteoroids.)

Briefly then, according to these methods, the universe and our galaxy would by 15 billion to 20 billion years old, the sun 5 billion to 10 billion years old and our solar system about 5 billion years old.

Geological Evidence: Radioactive

Geology also provides scientific evidence for the age of the earth. For convenience, we shall divide this evidence into radioactive evidence and nonradioactive evidence.

Among the more than 90 different chemical elements which occur naturally on the earth, there are a number which have unstable varieties or isotopes. An element is unstable if its nucleus has a tendency to break up spontaneously. This usually occurs by the shedding of a helium nucleus (alpha decay) or an electron (beta decay), with the result that the unstable nucleus changes into the nucleus of another element. The original radioactive element is called the *parent* element and the resultant nucleus, the *daughter* element. Thus, for example, the heavy isotope of carbon known as carbon-14 decays into (normal) nitrogen-14 by ejecting an electron.

The process of radioactive decay is understood reasonably well by physicists in terms of energy levels in the nucleus which are close enough to being unbound that the laws of quantum mechanics allow an occasional particle to escape. Though limitations on human knowledge due to Heisenberg's uncertainty principle do not permit prediction of the moment of decay for any single nucleus, yet it is possible to give statistical decay rates which are quite accurate for the enormous number of atomic nuclei found in the smallest chunks of mineral that can be studied chemically. Thus, no one can tell when a given carbon-14 nucleus will decay. But it is known that, given a large number of carbon-14 atoms, half of them will change to nitrogen-14 in about 5,730 years, the so-called half-life of carbon-14.[20]

Because radioactive decay involves only the energy levels in a nucleus and the potential energy barrier resulting from the interaction of its nuclear and electromagnetic forces, external forces will only influence the decay rate of a radioactive element if they are strong enough to be comparable to the nuclear force. Such forces are available at the center of the sun or at the "business end" of a manmade nuclear particle accelerator, but they are not to be found naturally anywhere on or in the earth. As there is evidence that nuclear forces are not changing with time,[21] the decay rate of a radioactive isotope should operate as a kind of clock by which to measure time.

Basically, the method of radioactive dating depends upon the fact that the number of decays of a given element is proportional to the number of atoms of the element present in the mineral sample. An equation relating the present number of atoms, N, of the parent element to its original amount, N_o (say, at the time the mineral crystallized), is as follows:

$$N = N_o \left(\tfrac{1}{2}\right)^{t/T_{1/2}}$$

where $t/T_{1/2}$ is the exponent of the fraction ½, $T_{1/2}$ is the so-called half-life of the element, and t is the time elapsed since the parent element consisted of its original amount, N_0. Then if N, N_0 and $T_{1/2}$ are known for a given element in a mineral sample, the elapsed time t (the age of the rock) can be found. $T_{1/2}$ can usually be measured accurately to a per cent or so in the laboratory and is fixed for a given decay scheme. For example, a few of the half-lives important to radioactive dating are:

Parent	Daughter	Half-life (in years)	Type of Decay[22]
Carbon-14	Nitrogen-14	5730	Beta
Potassium-40	Argon-40	1.3 billion	Electron Capture
Uranium-235	Lead-207	713 million	7 Alpha, 4 Beta
Uranium-238	Lead-206	4.5 billion	8 Alpha, 6 Beta
Rubidium-87	Strontium-87	47 billion	Beta

N can be measured by one of several types of chemical analysis. These, in practice, limit the accuracy of age determinations to values ranging from 1/10 to 10 times the half-life. But how may the original amount of the parent element, N_0, be found? If the chemical nature of the mineral involved is such that (1) the daughter element would not be crystallized into it originally, and (2) cannot escape from it subsequently, then $N_0 = N + D$, where D is the present amount (number of atoms) of the daughter element.

If these two conditions do not hold, then other means have to be used to determine N_0 or the sample cannot be dated. For the decay of carbon-14, the nitrogen daughter product is lost from most materials, so it is assumed that the carbon-14 in once-living samples (hair, cloth, bone, wood) was equal to its proportion in the atmosphere at the time the sample "died." This can be estimated from the fraction in our present atmosphere after subtracting the effects of atomic-weapon testing and fossil-fuel burning. Unfortunately, variations in the cosmic radiation which reaches our lower atmosphere (and produces carbon-14 from nitrogen-14) have occurred in the past, so that the carbon-14 method is not entirely reliable and must be calibrated by another dating method.[23]

For uranium decay, N_0 can be estimated by assuming that iron meteorites preserve the original ratios of lead isotopes uncontaminated by decay products. This is reasonable because uranium has very different chemical properties than the iron and nickel which compose these meteorites. Then the two uranium schemes can be used together on terrestrial rocks to show that they have been accumulating lead from decaying uranium for about 4.55 billion years. This is how the usual figure for the age of the earth is derived.[24] To measure the age of crystallization of rocks containing uranium and lead, the assumption about iron meteorites is unnecessary, but the two different uranium-lead decay schemes are used simultaneously. The chemical similarity of uranium-235 to uranium-238, and of lead-206 to lead-207, together with their divergent half-lives, protects the calculation against the loss of either parent or daughter elements, as neither parent element will be removed or added in preference to the other, nor will this occur with the daughter elements.[25]

Even in rocks where the daughter element was initially present, it is sometimes possible to estimate N_0. This can be done if there are two types of crystals in the rock, one containing the parent and daughter elements initially, and another containing only the daughter element originally. (The exclusion of the parent element from the daughter element at crystallization may have been due to the chemical nature of the parent element and the crystal.) The ratio of isotopes (including the daughter element) in these crystals which lack the parent element can then be used to subtract the original daughter element from the crystals which do contain the parent element, so that the amount of daughter element produced by decay is isolated. This procedure works well for the rubidium-strontium decay scheme in certain types of rocks.[26]

A special case of radioactive decay is the natural fission of uranium into two nearly equally heavy elements, with a half-life of about 10 million billion (10^{16}) years.[27] The recoil of the two daughter elements damages the crystal structure of the mineral in which the fission occurs. Etching a recently cut and polished surface of the mineral will display the damage as small tunnels. Other causes of such tunneling can be ruled out in most minerals, and the age of the rock (since it was last hot enough to destroy such tunnels by annealing) can be determined. Because chemical analysis is not necessary, this method is effective for times ranging from a century to over a billion years in the past.[28]

With the careful choice of minerals to be dated, the techniques described above allow the dating of many samples by two or more methods, thus providing convergent evidence of age. There are still uncertainties in radioactive dating, but the burden of proof seems to be upon those who claim that these methods are completely unreliable and that the earth is only a few thousand years old.

Geological Evidence: Nonradioactive

As radioactive dating methods have been developed only since the end of World War 2, the earliest methods used by geologists to date fossils, geologic strata and the whole earth were nonradioactive. No nonradioactive method has yet proved to be reliable for very ancient dates, although tree-ring dating, layered sedimentation in lake beds, thermoluminescence in flints and pottery, and racemization[29] of amino acids all show promise for dating more recent periods. Many phenomena can be cited, however, which do not fit well into a scheme which asserts that the earth or universe is quite young and the geologic strata were laid down in one or a few catastrophic events.

Appendix 1 provides a great deal of this data which is integral to the discussion of nonradioactive evidences of the age of the earth. It suggests that to view the earth as only a few thousand years old is scientifically untenable.

2

Evidence from the Solar System

The earth is one of nine presently-known planets which, together with thirty-three moons and many asteroids and comets, orbit an average star we call the sun and form the solar system. A number of striking details characterize this system and must be taken into account in any theory of the formation of the earth and the other planets.[1]

Mass and Angular Momentum

First of all, our solar system is unlike most known astronomical objects and systems in regard to the distribution of mass and angular momentum. Almost all the mass of our solar system is concentrated in the relatively miniscule volume occupied by the sun. Specifically, the mass of the sun is 750 times that of all the planets taken together (the mass of satellites, asteroids and comets is relatively insignificant), while the radius of the sun is only 1/8000 that of the solar system. Therefore, over 99.8 per cent of the mass of the solar system is concentrated in 2 trillionths of its volume! By contrast, the mass of a gas cloud, planet, star, star cluster or galaxy is much more uniformly distributed throughout its volume.

On the other hand, most of the angular momentum of the solar system is concentrated in the planets. Angular momentum is a useful measure of the quantity of rotation in an object or group of objects. In the simplest case, which applies to planets rotating about the sun, angular momentum is defined as the product of the planet's mass, orbital velocity and distance from the center of rotation (the sun). Computing the sun's angular momentum is more complex, but it is about 6 per cent of the product of its mass, rotational velocity at its surface and radius.[2] The sun has only about 0.5 per cent of the total angular momentum in the solar system, even though its surface is rotating at more than one mile per second at its equator. Again, the angular momentum of the other types of astronomical objects is more uniformly distributed.

This separation of mass and angular momentum in the solar system cannot be explained by gravity, the only significant force affecting the motion of the solar system today. Gravity is a so-called central force, acting directly between the centers of mass of two objects, and does not easily transfer angular momentum from one body to another. Therefore, a scientific model for the origin of the solar system must somehow account for the present disparity in the concentrations of mass and angular momentum in the solar system.

Orbital Regularity

Considering next the individual motions of the various objects which constitute the solar system, some striking regularities present themselves. The orbits of the planets, for instance, are very regular, particularly when contrasted with the orbits of the comets. All nine planets move around the sun in the same direction. Their orbits are nearly circular, and they lie nearly in the same plane. Table 1 gives the eccentricity and tilt of each planetary orbit.

Eccentricity measures the shape of the planetary orbit, which, by Kepler's First Law, is an ellipse. An eccentricity of zero indicates a circular orbit. Values between zero and one indicate ellipses with elongation increasing with the eccentricity. An eccentricity of one denotes an "ellipse" squashed into a straight line. Notice in Table 1 that all but two of the planetary orbits have eccentricities under 0.100 and none are more than 0.250. Comets, by contrast, have much more elongated orbits, with eccentricities usually in excess of 0.500.[3]

Regularity of Planetary Orbits: Their Eccentricities and the Inclination of Their Orbital Planes with Respect to the Earth's Plane

Planet	Eccentricity	Inclination
Mercury	.206	7.0°
Venus	.007	3.4°
Earth	.017	—
Mars	.093	1.9°
Jupiter	.048	1.3°
Saturn	.056	2.5°
Uranus	.047	0.8°
Neptune	.009	1.8°
Pluto	.249	17.2°

Source: Robert H. Baker and Laurence W. Frederick, *Astronomy*, 9th ed. (New York: D. Van Nostrand Company, 1971), p. 590.

Table 1

Each planetary orbit, being an ellipse, describes a plane. These planes are very nearly aligned, as shown in the third column of Table 1. Only two planets have tilts larger than 3.5 degrees, and these are the innermost and outermost planets, Mercury and Pluto respectively. As we shall see in the next chapter, this regularity places a strong restriction on feasible models for the origin of the solar system.

The orbital regularity of the planets is accompanied by certain irregularities involving less energy and motions on a smaller scale. The rotations of the planets on their own axes and the movements of the satellites about the planets are far less regular than the rotation of the planets about the sun. This may suggest that forces weaker and of shorter range have disrupted the uniformity produced by a stronger long-range force.

Chemical Evidence

The chemistry of the solar system also forms a significant class of data which may relate to origins.[4] The sun, a massive sphere of gas, consists mostly of hydrogen (80 per cent) and a large minority of helium (18 per cent), leaving only a small fraction (2 per cent) for all the heavier elements. Earth, however, has comparatively little hydrogen or helium, and is primarily composed of the heavier elements which for the most part are found in similar relative proportions on the sun.

Moreover, the planets fall into two distinct chemical groups. The inner planets (Mercury, Venus, Earth, Mars) are small compared to the outer planets (Jupiter, Saturn, Uranus, Neptune),[5] but they have a density four times as great, or about five times that of water. The greater size and lesser density of the outer planets indicate that they contain a larger fraction of hydrogen and helium than do the inner planets, yet a smaller fraction than is found in the sun.

Hydrogen and helium and, to a lesser extent, the common hydrogen compounds water (H_2O), ammonia (NH_3) and methane (CH_4) are more volatile than the metals and silicates which are the principal components of the inner planets. But how did most of the volatile materials come to be at the center (sun) and the outside (outer planets) of the solar system with only a little in between? This problem, too, places a severe constraint on any theory for the origin of the solar system. The model should answer this question.

Turning to the earth in particular, what sort of data must a model for its origin fit? Seismology, the study of earthquakes, indicates that the earth is composed of roughly spherical layers, like an onion.[6] There is a solid inner core and a liquid outer core, both of which are very dense. By analogy with meteorites, it is thought that the earth's core is metallic, an alloy principally of iron and nickel. The flow of material in the liquid part of the core would generate electric currents to produce the earth's magnetic field.[7]

Above the core are several layers which form a thick region called the mantle. The mantle is a solid which is very close to being liquid, roughly like asphalt or "silly-putty." As a result, it behaves as a solid in reaction to rapidly changing forces such as earthquakes, but will flow under the influence of long-term forces. Chemically, the mantle is more akin to our surface rocks than it is to the core, for it appears to consist of various metals compounded with silicon and oxygen. Its density is intermediate to that of average surface rocks and the core. The mantle evidently carries heat outward from the earth's interior by means of slow convection currents (the hotter material rises, the cooler sinks) which, incidentally, cause the continents and sea floors to drift slowly along the surface of the earth.[8]

At the earth's surface is a thin layer of solid rock called the crust. This crust is of two types. One is rich in silicon-aluminum compounds, forms the continents, and may be as much as 35 miles thick in places. The other, a heavier sort, underlies the continents, is richer in silicon-magnesium compounds, and forms the ocean basins where the crust is sometimes as little as 4 to 5 miles thick.

Over the crust are the oceans, covering two-thirds of the earth's surface to an average depth of nearly three miles. If the crust were smoothed out to remove all height variations, the whole earth would be covered by about two miles of water!

Above the earth's surface is another "ocean," of air, which gradually thins out to blend with the solar "atmosphere" several hundred miles up. Earth's atmosphere is mostly nitrogen (78 per cent) with a large fraction of oxygen (21 per cent) and about 1 per cent of heavier gases. These percentages neglect small but locally varying amounts of dust, water vapor and carbon dioxide. The other inner planets about which we have substantial atmospheric information, Mars and Venus, seem to have carbon dioxide in place of Earth's oxygen. Free water also seems to be scarce on the other inner planets, and they have weak and insignificant magnetic fields.[9]

With this brief sketch of the principal features of the solar system as a whole and of Earth in particular, let us now look at the various scientific models which seek to account for these features in terms of planetary origins.

3

Selecting a Model

Let us concentrate first on the nature of the solar system as a whole and attempt to select a "best theory" to explain its features. Following that, we shall consider details in the history of Earth as a separate planet.

In the past two centuries, many theories have been proposed for the origin of the solar system.[1] Basically the models proposed fall into three classes: (1) the planets, or the material from which the planets were later formed, were captured by our sun from interstellar space; (2) the planetary material was pulled from our sun by a passing star; and (3) the planets and the sun formed simultaneously from the same cloud of condensing interstellar matter. Let us examine each type of theory in turn.

Interstellar Capture Theories

There are two subclasses of this alternative. In the first, which we may call planetary capture theories, the planets were originally formed somewhere beyond our solar system by an unknown process. After traveling for ages through space, the planets were captured into orbits around the sun. This theory has been advocated by the Christian author Donald Patten,[2] and apparently by the controversial Immanuel Velikovsky.[3] These models do not explain the origin of planets, they merely remove the process from our locality. Another model must then be invoked to explain the origin of planets as such.

An additional problem that such models face is the fact that one planet cannot be captured into an orbit by a single star. Two objects which are gravitationally attracted to each other cannot switch from an open configuration to a closed one without the help of a third body. Thus we must postulate one of the following: (a) the sun already had a planet in orbit around it when the first planet to be captured approached (which contradicts the "ground rules" of this class of models); (b) the sun had another star in orbit with it; (c) the planet was orbiting another star which passed close to the sun (a variety of the second class of solar system theories mentioned above); or (d) two or more planets, traveling together, encountered the sun and one or more of them were captured.

In spite of the variety of these models, they all are inadequate to explain the great regularity in the planetary orbits. Assuming that such captures would give random orbital planes for the captured planets, there is only one chance in 10 million billion billion (10^{25}) that the alignment of these orbital planes we actually observe would occur.[4]

Even if it is supposed that the orbital planes of the planets are more likely to be aligned because several planets were captured simultaneously or because, once the first planet has been captured, there is a higher probability for capture in the plane of that planet, there is still the problem of the circularity of the planetary orbits. If the planets were captured already formed (rather than as dust particles), there is no mechanism available to circularize what would normally be highly elongated orbits, in the short times required by Velikovsky and Patten. The chance that the orbits would just happen to be circular when the planets were captured, or that they would become as circular as they are by near collisions among one another is roughly one in a million million (10^{12}).[5] Consequently, this whole subclass of theories is unsatisfactory as an explanation for the origin of our planetary system.

The other subclass of this first class of models suggests that our planets were captured from interstellar space in the form of dust and gas, rather than as whole planets. This vastly increases the number of collisions that would occur in the captured material, thereby making most likely the production of circular orbits in a single plane.[6] One problem with such views, however, is the fact that the sun's equator is only seven degrees from the plane of the planetary orbits. There is only one chance in 250 of such a close alignment, which suggests that it is not accidental. In addition, this type of theory does not account for the unusually small angular momentum of the sun relative to the solar system as a whole or to the gas cloud from which the sun would presumably have formed. Most astronomers, therefore, prefer another theory for the origin of the solar system.[7]

Close Approach Theories

Another class of models, in which our planets are the result of a near-collision between our sun and another star, was popular into the 1950s. T. C. Chamberlin, F. R. Moulton and Sir James Jeans are most closely associated with views of this sort. As two stars approach one another, tides are raised in the gaseous material of which they are composed. If the stars happen to pass extremely close to each other, some of this gas is pulled so far from its parent star as to go out into orbit. After the stars separate, it was supposed, this material would cool off and eventually condense into planets.

This model is superior to the planetary capture theory, for it predicts that the orbits will lie in a single plane (that described by the movement of the two stars). This plane might be expected to be near the plane of the sun's equator, because the solar rotation would surely have been influenced by a close encounter with another star. However, the sudden pull exerted by a star passing this close to the sun would bring the solar material out into space very quickly, and the hot gas would disperse instead of condensing to form planets. In any case, the orbits of this material would be very elongated, and the stars would probably soon recapture it.[8]

Even if these difficulties could be surmounted, according to the close-approach model, planetary systems would be very rare, for the stars in our galaxy are widely spaced. Statistical calculations indicate that only a few hundred of the near-collisions needed to extract gas from a star would have occurred in our galaxy since it formed. Recent evidence, however, indicates that planetary systems are much more common than this, perhaps being a feature of most single stars.[9] Therefore, this model, too, is inadequate to account for the origin of the solar system.

Star Formation Models

The third class of models views the planets as natural byproducts in the formation of a single star as it condenses from a cloud of interstellar gas and dust. This type of theory was first proposed by Immanuel Kant (late in the eighteenth century) and Pierre Laplace (early in the nineteenth century). A vast increase in our observational data and theoretical understanding has produced numerous modifications and revisions since then, yet some variety of this view is held by most investigators today.[10]

We shall discuss in some detail the particular view of

Thomas Gold and Fred Hoyle,[11] as it seems to fit the whole range of data better than its competitors. The principal difference between this model and the other star-formation views is the introduction of a magnetic field to solve the angular momentum problem.

Gravity has the longest range among known forces. Its effect decreases inversely with the square of the distance between the masses involved. Unlike the electromagnetic force, gravity cannot be neutralized because it is produced by a quantity called mass which is only positive, rather than positive and negative like electric charges. As a result, gravity is the dominant force in the movement of astronomical bodies of substantial size.

Even if one supposes that negative masses are lurking somewhere in the depths of space, the electric and gravitational forces are still not analogous, for like charges repel, whereas like masses attract. Systems of particles dominated by the force of gravity are unstable and tend to contract.

As we look out into the space between the stars, we find that there is no strict vacuum here, even though we cannot produce a better vacuum on earth. Instead, interstellar space is "filled" with clouds of gas and dust, some so thin as to be invisible, others thick enough to scatter or completely absorb the light from stars lying beyond them.

No matter how low the density of such a gas cloud, if it is not too hot and has enough mass, the mutual gravitation of the gas particles (atoms or molecules) will overcome the gas pressure and the cloud will contract. The higher the average density of the cloud, the less mass it need have to collapse. External forces, such as magnetic fields or shock waves, may aid in starting such a collapse.[12]

According to the big bang cosmology, mentioned in chapter 1, the universe began with matter and energy concentrated in a hot mass which expanded explosively. Condensation of gas clouds would occur as soon as the temperature had dropped to a sufficiently low value (due to this general expansion) for self-gravitation to overcome the expansion. This would first occur only for very large volumes, so that large-scale clouds would be formed. But as these became denser due to their own contraction, each large cloud would split into smaller ones, which, after further contraction, would divide into even smaller clouds.[13] In this way, it appears, the observed hierarchical structure of the universe was formed: stars occur in clusters, clusters in galaxies, and galaxies themselves are grouped in clusters and perhaps superclusters.[14]

Turning now to the relatively small cloud which would eventually contract to form our sun and its planets, let us consider the forces which are at work in the cloud. First, and strongest, is the inwardly-directed gravitational force which produces the contraction. The strength of this force depends on the distribution of the dust and gas within the cloud.

Resisting this gravitational contraction is the gas pressure, which depends on the temperature and density of the gas at each point in the cloud. As the cloud contracts, both the temperature and density rise due to compression, but the loss of energy from the cloud by radiation keeps the temperature from rising rapidly enough to stop the contraction. Only the sudden onset of nuclear fusion, when the central temperature of the cloud reaches about 10 million degrees Kelvin, provides a heat source powerful enough to counteract the gravitational contraction, thereby producing a star.[15]

Returning to early stages of the contraction, let us examine more specifically this development. The gas cloud or *protosun* would have been tenuous enough to be transparent. A hypothetical observer located inside the cloud would be able to look out of it with no difficulty. Any stars in existence at that time (since the sun appears to be at least a second-generation star[16]) would be visible. As the contraction proceeds, however, the gas and dust would eventually become dense enough to scatter and then to absorb all light from outside, so that the cloud would become dark everywhere within.

Other processes are also going on as the cloud contracts. Collisions between gas atoms or molecules tend to cancel out all but two of the large-scale motions. Of the two remaining motions, (1) the linear movement of the cloud through space and (2) its rotation, the latter is more significant for the further development of the cloud.

The continued contraction of the cloud amplifies this rotation in the same way that the drawing in of the arms toward the body increases a figure skater's rate of spin. Both cases demonstrate the conservation of angular momentum. But rotation produces a third force, called *centrifugal*, which is directed outward and is strongest at the "equator" of the cloud. The strength of the centrifugal force increases with the rate of rotation. As a result, the cloud collapses more slowly near its equator than near its poles, and its shape become flatter. If this effect were not eventually hindered, the cloud would become pancake-shaped rather than spherical (see figure 3).

The collapse of a gas cloud to form a star involves an enormous contraction. The cloud is typically on the order of a light-year (6 trillion miles) across when it breaks away from the surrounding clouds, but the star's diameter when the contraction stops is only about a million miles. If the angular momentum normally present in the original cloud were concentrated in the final star, it would split apart. Therefore, few stars could form without shedding some of their angular momentum.

If the angular momentum of a cloud is sufficiently high, it will split into pieces before proceeding to the next stage, and a multiple star system will be produced. In such a case, the production of planets is less likely because multiple stars allow for fewer stable planetary orbits.

Meanwhile the temperature of the gas cloud rises as potential energy is converted into heat as well as into radiation.[17] As the cloud gets hotter, the wavelength of its radiated energy becomes shorter, until finally the cloud begins to glow visibly. At this point, our hypothetical observer inside the cloud would see everything around him glowing. It appears that this transition from "no glow" to "glow" would occur in a matter of months, very quickly on the astronomical time-scale.

The glowing of our gas cloud also signals the beginning of substantial ionization. At temperatures of several thousand degrees, the collision of atoms in the cloud is sufficiently violent to rip off electrons, changing the gas into an ionized plasma, sometimes considered a fourth state of matter distinct from solid, liquid or gas.[18]

The appearance of ionization among the three forces already struggling in the collapsing cloud introduces a fourth force, electromagnetism, which is generated by the electrically charged ions and electrons. Up to this point, the struggle between gravity and gas pressure would have produced

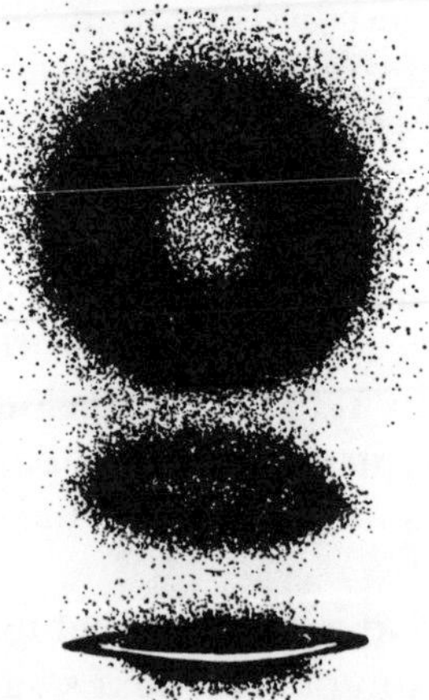

Figure 3. Stages in the collapse of a gas cloud to form a star and planets. The narrow equatorial band is produced when the gas becomes ionized and magnetic forces are introduced. Adapted from Fred Hoyle, *Astronomy* (Garden City: Doubleday, 1962), p. 270.

Figure 4. Magnetic lines of force, behaving somewhat like rubber bands transmit faster rotation to the outer part of the gas cloud while slowing down the rotation of the inner part. Adapted from Fred Hoyle, *Astronomy* (Garden City: Doubleday, 1962), p. 271.

a roughly spherical cloud, but the presence of rotation tended to counteract the gravitational collapse near the cloud's equator to produce a shape called in mathematics an oblate spheroid (less technically, the shape of an M&M chocolate candy, non-peanut type), which gradually flattened as the cloud collapsed.

Now, however, we have a plasma filled with a tangle of magnetic fields which, somewhat like rubber bands, resist stretching. With the plasma densities and linear dimensions involved here, the magnetic field is said to be "frozen-in," so that the motion of the plasma carries the field with it, and the movement of the field moves the plasma.[19]

But the inner part of the cloud, with higher density, is already rotating more rapidly than the outer part, so that any magnetic fields connecting the two regions tend to get stretched. Resisting this stretching, the magnetic field lines slow up the rotation of the inner region and speed up that of the outer region (see figure 4). As a result, the inner region has less centrifugal force to contend with and it begins to collapse more rapidly and return to a more spherical shape. The outer region, however, now has more centrifugal force applied to it and it becomes more flattened.

In fact, the combination of pressure and increased centrifugal force now overcomes the inward pull of gravity near the cloud's equator in this outer region with the result that the flattened outer region begins to move radially outward in the equatorial plane of the cloud, so that the whole cloud begins to look something like Saturn with its rings. In this way, angular momentum is transferred from the central mass, which will eventually form the sun, to a flat disk of ionized gas and dust rotating in the same direction as the cloud, which will later form the planets (see figure 3).

As this outward-moving ring of material gets away from the glowing central gas cloud, it begins to cool off and become un-ionized. For the small fraction of heavier elements in the ring, this occurs relatively close to the cloud, whereas the more volatile elements or compounds do not regain their electrical neutrality until they have moved farther out. When the material is no longer ionized, it "unhooks" from the magnetic field and ceases to move outward, taking up circular orbits around the protosun.

The gas cloud-protosun still continues to collapse, perhaps repeating several times the process of throwing off angular momentum by means of a ring of material. Such rings and the remaining cloud may have slightly different planes of rotation due to small differences in the detailed distribution of mass, angular momentum and magnetic fields in the collapsing cloud.

Finally the cloud has, by continual collapse, become sufficiently hot at its center for a nuclear fusion reaction to begin. The conversion of hydrogen into helium produces sufficient heat to cause the gas pressure to balance the force of gravity, stopping the collapse as long as the hydrogen fuel can maintain the heat (see pp. 22-23).

Meanwhile, the less volatile materials in the ring or rings of gas have condensed into small solid particles with various liquids and gases adsorbed on their surfaces. Because this material lies in a thin disk, it conglomerates rather quickly into planet-sized objects, perhaps in as little as ten thousand years.[20] Contrary to earlier views, in which each planet was thought to have been a large individual gas cloud which cooled to a molten ball and then solidified, it now appears that the planets were formed "cold," from the collision of solid dust particles.[21]

Near the end of this process, there would be a number of rather violent collisions, as the larger competitors in each orbital area "fought it out" for final control. Thus the presence of massive Jupiter seems to have interfered with the formation of a planet in the present asteroid belt, and it probably captured considerable material which would otherwise have gone to form Mars. These collisions would also be responsible for the disorder in the small-scale motions of the solar system, such as the rotation of the planets on their axes. Asteroid-sized objects colliding with the nearly full-sized planets would modify their angular momentum with respect to their own axes of rotation.[22]

The Development of the Earth

Focusing now on the newly-formed earth, we would find a lifeless sphere of conglomerated nonvolatile compounds, with hydrates, liquids and gases loosely attached. There would be no oceans nor any atmosphere to speak of. The interior, though rather warm due to the high pressure of overlying materials, probably would not be nearly as hot as at present.[23]

But radioactive elements with short half-lives would soon begin to heat the interior. Since the earth is a rather good insulator, its internal temperature would rise, melting some materials, breaking down many compounds, and driving off the hydrates and adsorbed gases and liquids. Lighter materials, such as water and various gases, would seek the surface, whereas the heavier materials such as iron and nickel would flow downward to form the core. Gradually the earth would come to have the various layers we see today.[24]

As the water and gases reached the surface, an atmosphere and ocean would be formed. If the gases spewed out by volcanoes today[25] and the atmospheres of Venus and Mars provide reliable clues,[26] then the early terrestrial atmosphere would have had little or no free oxygen. Instead the oxygen would have been locked up in carbon dioxide. As a result, the atmosphere would have been more effective in trapping heat from the sun (the so-called greenhouse effect), so that the surface temperatures would have been higher, more water would have vaporized and the cloud cover would have been much thicker than it is today. Yet a glance at pictures of the earth taken from space shows that a moderate increase in our present cloud cover would make it impossible to see any astronomical objects, even though a large amount of diffuse sunlight might reach the surface.

Sometime later in the earth's history, an event occurred to change the atmosphere. Von R. Eshleman, commenting on the differences between the present atmospheres of Earth, Venus and Mars, suggests that plant life on the earth has replaced most of our carbon dioxide by oxygen.[27] This would decrease the greenhouse effect, lower the temperature, precipitate much of the water vapor and tend to clear up the atmosphere.

As for the oceans, they presently contain enough water to cover the earth's surface to a depth of two miles if the surface were perfectly flat. As a matter of fact, however, the surface of the earth today has enough relief that the oceans cover only two-thirds of the surface, while one-third remains above water. But continental drift (or, more accurately, the movement of crustal plates) is thought to be responsible for the formation of mountains and for opening deep ocean basins between continents.[28] In addition, most areas of the earth contain marine fossils, and all the earliest fossils are of marine life. All this suggests that the surface relief of the solid earth was once small enough for a single ocean to cover the entire planet.

Volcanic action such as we see forming islands in the Atlantic and Pacific (but on a larger scale) would eventually have formed large islands, called continental shields. Continued erosion and metamorphosis of these islands would have separated heavier, more soluble *simatic* materials (dominated by silicon and magnesium) from the lighter, less soluble *sialic* (dominated by silicon and aluminum), so that the latter would be left to form the bulk of the continents we observe today.[29]

This chapter has sketched a model for the origin of the earth and solar system which explains (1) the regular orbital characteristics of the planets, as well as (2) the smaller-scale irregularities in their rotational motion and that of their moons; (3) the unusual distribution of mass and angular momentum in the solar system; and (4) the chemical make-up of the system in which the sun and outer planets are composed largely of volatile materials, whereas the inner planets are mostly nonvolatile. We have also appended a brief resume of the formation and early history of the earth as best we can discern the situation from scientific evidence available today.

It is now appropriate to compare this scientific evidence with that of the biblical materials.

Part II
Theology

4

Chronological Evidence from Scripture

What is the biblical teaching on the age of the earth? The answer is commonly assumed, both in Christian and non-Christian circles, to be quite clearly only a few thousand years. After all, this is certainly the ancient, traditional though not unanimous position. Even before the time of Christ, Jewish writings such as the book of Jubilees proclaimed such a view.[1] A number of early Christian writers make explicit statements that human history lasts only a few millennia.[2] Later, Archbishop Ussher (1581-1656) fixed the date of creation at 4004 B.C.[3] and Dr. John Lightfoot (1602-75) went so far as to name the day and hour![4]

Basically, there are two lines of argument for a relatively young earth which use the biblical material. First, it is asserted that the genealogies in Genesis 5 and 11 do not allow for more than a few thousand years from Adam to Abraham. Second, the creation account itself teaches that Adam is only a day younger than the oldest animals, and less than a week younger than the universe. Let us examine each of these arguments in turn.

The Genesis Genealogies

The argument for a young earth based on the genealogies in Genesis 5 and 11 runs basically as follows. The approximate dates for the life of Abraham obtained from the biblical data and archaeology are 2000 B.C. to 1700 B.C. But Abraham is in the last generation listed in the genealogy of Genesis 11. Since this genealogy gives the age of each father at the birth of his son, we can calculate the time elapsed from the birth of Shem (the first mentioned in the Genesis 11 list) to the birth of Abraham as 390 years.

Similarly, Shem is in the last generation in the genealogy

Genealogy in Genesis Eleven		Genealogy in Genesis Five	
Name	**Age at birth of son**	**Name**	**Age at birth of son**
Shem	100	Adam	130
Arpachshad	35	Seth	105
Shelah	30	Enosh	90
Eber	34	Kenan	70
Peleg	30	Mahalalel	65
Reu	32	Jared	162
Serug	30	Enoch	65
Nahor	29	Methuselah	187
Terah	70	Lamech	182
Abraham	—	Noah	500
		Shem	—
Table 2		**Table 3**	

in Genesis 5. Here, too, we have the age of each father at the birth of his son, and therefore we can calculate the time elapsed from the creation of Adam to the birth of Shem, namely 1,556 years.

Adding the figures obtained from both genealogies, the total elapsed time from Adam to Abraham is 1,946 years. This figure added to the known approximate date for Abraham results in the conclusion that Adam was created about 4000 B.C. or slightly more recently.

But is this the teaching of Scripture, or is it merely an inference which may be mistaken? The writers of Scripture nowhere make such a calculation themselves, nor do they explicitly indicate the purpose of these genealogies.

Late in the nineteenth century, when Princeton Seminary was still defending the inerrancy of Scripture, William Henry Green, professor of Old Testament there, wrote an excellent article on genealogies.[5] This article is reprinted here as appendix 2. Briefly, the points made by Professor Green are:

1. By a comparison of the genealogies which appear in Scripture, it is apparent that omission of unimportant names from such lists is the rule rather than the exception.
2. Even the use of the terms "father," "son" and "begot" may be shown from scriptural usage to be far broader than we might expect. They are often used for persons related at a distance of several generations, and sometimes even of persons not physically related at all.
3. It is not unprecedented for Scripture to pass over very long periods of time with little or no remark.
4. The records of Egyptian civilization seem to preclude a date for the flood in line with the genealogical calculations made above (about 2300 B.C.).
5. The genealogies of Genesis 5 and 11 have a symmetry which suggests intentional arrangement.

Professor Green makes a number of additional comments of significance. We recommend that you read his paper in full at this point. His paper closes with the following statement:

> On these various grounds we conclude that the Scriptures furnish no data for a chronological computation prior to the life of Abraham; and that the Mosaic records do not fix and were not intended to fix the precise date either of the Flood or of the creation of the world.

Noted proponents of a recent creation, such as John C. Whitcomb, Jr. and Henry M. Morris, have felt the strength of Green's arguments and the evidence of archaeology to the extent of revising the date of creation back to 10,000 B.C. or so, but they have felt that further concessions would make the gaps between names in the genealogies too large.[6] Although one has some sympathy for this feeling, it is not based on any specific exegetical data. The Bible does not specify the date of creation, whether of the universe or of man. Therefore, information on this question must be obtained elsewhere, presumably through scientific investigation.

Incidentally, it is interesting to note that certain passages of Scripture fit especially well into the view that creation occurred much more than a few thousand years ago. In several passages the "last days" or "last times" are seen as starting with the first coming of the Messiah (Acts 2:17; Heb. 1:2; 1 Pet. 1:20). Using almost exactly the same terminology as is found in Matthew 28:20, Hebrews 9:26 says that Jesus appeared once "at *the end of the age* to put away sin by the sacrifice of himself" (my emphasis). The Apostle John, writing near the end of the first century, tells his readers that it is already "the last hour" (1 Jn. 2:18). But these expressions hardly make sense if 20 to 33 per cent of human history was yet to intervene. Likewise, Jesus' frequent promises to come soon (for example, Rev. 1:3; 21:10, 12, 20) are more easily understood if mankind had lived in sin for tens or hundreds of thousands of years before his first coming.

The Length of the Creation Period

Even granting that creation may have taken place a long time ago, is there not disagreement between the Bible and science on the length of time which elapsed between the beginning of the universe and the appearance of man? Indeed, there is disagreement between some models constructed using the biblical data and some using the scientific data. But does the Bible really teach that man is only a few days younger than the universe?

Essentially, the argument in favor of a short creation period is that creation took place in six consecutive days and that the literal meaning of "day" is a twenty-four-hour period. Let us examine this argument.

An elaborate word study of the Hebrew *yom* ("day") is not necessary to show that it is used rather like our English word "day." Often it means a period of activity during which the sun is up, roughly twelve hours long, depending on the season (Gen. 1:5; 1:14a). At other times it represents a day-night pair, a twenty-four-hour day (Gen. 1:14b; Num. 3:13). Less frequently it is used for longer periods of time (Gen. 2:4; Eccl. 12:3). Which of these usages should be called "literal" and which "figurative" is somewhat a matter of semantics. In any case, the claim that *yom* always means a twenty-four-hour day cannot be substantiated by a survey of its actual use.

Neither can one prove that *yom*, when used with a number, takes on the more restricted idea of a twenty-four-hour day. Zechariah 14:7, it appears, speaks of the day of the Lord as a continuing period of time, and uses exactly the same Hebrew construction as is used for the "first day" in Genesis 1:5. The more modest claim, that *yom* means a twenty-four-hour day when used with *ordinal* numbers (1st, 2nd, 3rd, etc.), has the advantage that no clear counter-example can be cited with *yom* meaning a long period of time. The force of this observation is greatly reduced, however, when one considers that the Bible has no occasion to mention several long periods of time which might be numbered, except the days of creation. In any case, it is not clear why an adjective such as an ordinal number should change the range of meaning of the noun *yom*.

Concerning the question of which usages of *yom* are "literal" and which "figurative," the dictum "always take the literal meaning where possible" should not be used to rule out an alternative interpretation. Such a methodology, indeed, may be employed, but merely deciding to adopt the more common meaning of a word can only give a result which is *probable*, not one which is certain, and such interpretations should give way to any real contextual evidence available.

Is there any contextual evidence on the length of the creation period? The reference to creation in Exodus 20:8-11 has often been brought forward to prove that the creation week consisted of seven consecutive twenty-four-hour days:

> Remember the sabbath day, to keep it holy. Six days you shall labor and do all your work, but the seventh day is a sabbath of the LORD your God; in it you shall not do any work, you or your son or your daughter, your male or your female servant or your cattle or your sojourner who stays with you. For in six days the LORD made the heavens and the earth, the sea and all that is in them, and rested on the seventh day; therefore the LORD blessed the sabbath day and made it holy.

Because the Sabbath is a twenty-four-hour day (the argument goes) which is preceded by six consecutive twenty-four-hour work days, so creation week consisted of consecutive twenty-four-hour days.

This argument, however, is not necessarily valid, because it is an argument from analogy, not from identity. The work-week and Sabbath day differ from the creation week in *at least* one point—the former are repeated again and again, but the latter is not. Since the passage does not explicitly say that "day" is to be understood the same way in both cases, this may differ also, just as Protestants will agree that the "blood" we drink in the Lord's Supper is different from the blood he shed on Calvary, that the baptism we experience as we enter the church is different from the "baptism" Jesus experienced (Lk. 12:50), although our human activities in these cases commemorate God's activity. Perhaps twenty-four-hour days are used in the work-week to commemorate long periods in creation week.

It should not be forgotten that God also established two other kinds of sabbath: a year-long sabbath rest for the land following six years of use (Ex. 23:10-11; Lev. 25: 3-7) and a jubilee sabbath of disputed length (a few days to a year, Lev. 25:8-17) following "seven weeks of years." These examples should at least instruct us to pause and reflect before claiming that Exodus 20:8-11 proves the creation week consisted of seven consecutive twenty-four-hour days.

R. John Snow has examined the events of creation week usually assigned to the sixth day, and he has shown that a much longer period seems to be implied by the context. According to Genesis 1:24-31, the land animals and man were created on the sixth day (if it is proper to assign all the activities listed between the mention of the fifth day in 1:23 and of the sixth day in 1:31 to the latter day, as has traditionally been done).

Genesis 2 gives us an expanded view of God's activity in creating man. We see that the following activities must be assigned to day six according to the traditional view:

1. Land animals were created.
2. Adam was created.
3. God planted a garden in Eden.
4. God brought all animals before Adam, who named them.

5. God put Adam to sleep and constructed Eve from his side.

This series of events is very difficult to reconcile with a twenty-four-hour day, and Reverend Snow also shows that the Hebrew word translated "now" in the KJV and NASB (Gen. 2:23) actually has the force of "at last" and suggests a much longer period of time than is usually given for this sequence. Snow's paper, "How Long Is the Sixth Day?" is printed here as Appendix 3.

How is this dilemma to be handled? There are several solutions within the twenty-four-hour time frame: First, though the creation week is still composed of seven consecutive twenty-four-hour days, man before his fall could think far more rapidly than he can now. Therefore naming a few thousand animals in a few hours, even if their names reflect their character, was within the range of his ability. To this we respond following Snow, "Would Adam also become lonely more quickly than fallen man?" It appears that God did not seek to remedy Adam's being alone until sometime after Adam became aware of it.

The second solution is that the creation of woman did not occur during the first week, but during the second. This peculiar, old view is found in a Jewish work written before the time of Christ known as the book of Jubilees (3:1-6). It requires an unusual interpretation of "male and female" in Genesis 1:27, taking Adam to have been bisexual for one week. It also ignores the plural "them" in the same verse.

According to the third solution, the days of Genesis 1 are the twenty-four-hour kind, but they are not consecutive. Furthermore, it is *not* on these days that all the creative activity takes place, for then the "sixth-day problem" is still not solved. Rather the days serve some other purpose. It is my (R. C. Newman) suggestion that each day *opens* a new creative period (see figure 5), and therefore each day is mentioned in Genesis 1 after the activities of the previous creative period have been described, but before those of the next period are given. This suggestion will be discussed further in the following chapters.

Creative Period N (continues beyond Day N)		
	Day N	Creative Period N + 1 (starts with Day N)

Figure 5: Relation of days and creative periods in modified intermittent-day view

The sixth-day dilemma also can be solved by taking the days to be long periods of time, the so-called day-age view. This has been the most common solution adopted by proponents of progressive creationism, although overlapping "days" must be employed to fit fruit trees, which first appear in the fossil record after many of the land animals, but show up in the Genesis account on the fourth day, two days before land animals.

There is yet further evidence from the Scripture which favors models other than the creation week of seven consecutive, twenty-four-hour days. The fourth chapter of Hebrews tells us that believers can still enter into the rest of God mentioned in Genesis 2:2. This may be understood figuratively to mean that we, too, can someday rest just as God did long ago. But a more literal interpretation of the passage could suggest either that God is still resting (day-age view) and we are living now in the seventh day, or that God has not yet *begun* to rest as the seventh day is still in the future. I favor the latter suggestion on the basis of Jesus' answer to the Pharisees in John 5:17. When Jesus was attacked for healing a sick man on the Sabbath, he answered, "My Father is working still, and I am working." This is most easily understood as a serious answer to his opponents' charges if God has not yet completed his work of creation, a view which is thoroughly consistent with the evangelical belief that the regeneration of sinners is a creative activity of God. I suggest that we are living in the creative period which intervenes between the sixth and seventh days, and that God's activity in this period is principally the creation of a redeemed mankind (see figure 6, p. 84).

Having attempted to show that the exegetical support for a young earth created in six consecutive, twenty-four-hour days a few thousand years ago is inconclusive and overlooks important biblical data, we now turn to an examination of the detailed material on creation to be found in Scripture.

5

Genesis One

The basic source of biblical information on creation is the first two chapters of the book of Genesis. For our more restricted concern, which is largely nonbiological, the first nineteen verses of Genesis 1 are primary. In this chapter we shall consider these verses in order, note what is actually said in the Hebrew text and what range of interpretation is allowed thereby, and propose an interpretation.

Genesis 1:1

In the beginning God created the heavens and the earth. The dispute between conservatives and liberals over the significance of Genesis 1:1 is an old one. Liberals often regard the verse as a temporal clause. This removes from serious consideration the doctrine of creation *ex nihilo* (from no previously existing material). That is, they translate Genesis 1:1, "In the beginning when God created the heavens and the earth, the earth was without form. . . ." When so translated, the verse suggests that when God created he used chaotic matter which (presumably) had always existed. According to the liberal model, the doctrine of creation out of nothing (which was known to and unique to the Judeo-Christian tradition[1]) must have been a gigantic mistake which fortuitously advanced religion to a higher plane. Because this interpretation depends on an unusual Hebrew construction, is in disagreement with the Septuagint (Greek translation of the Old Testament) and fits the scientific evidence less satisfactorily than the traditional translation,[2] we shall pass over it to other alternatives.[3]

Two other interpretations of this verse are common. Some feel that Genesis 1:1 is a summary of the account to follow. In this case the book of Genesis begins, in effect, "All things began when God made the universe. Let me tell you about it. Now the earth was formless. . . ." But if this is the proper interpretation, there is a strange discontinuity between Genesis 1:1 and 1:2, for the former tells us that we are about to hear of God's creating the earth, but the latter presupposes the earth as already existing! This can be avoided by understanding "earth" in verse 2 to mean the formless matter from which the planet Earth will later be made. But this merely exchanges one problem for another, for then either the origin of matter remains a mystery or it is assumed that matter has always existed. It is true, of course, that the Bible does not tell us as much as we might like to know about certain subjects (for example, the fall of Satan, the fate of animals, or, in this case, the origin of matter). Nevertheless, it clearly teaches that everything but God is directly or remotely God-created. (Compare Genesis 1:1 with John 1:1-3.)

It seems more natural to the text to understand Genesis 1:1 as the first event of the creation sequence rather than as a temporal clause or a summary of what is to follow, for the next verse speaks of an earth as already existing in some sense. Verse 1 is presumably a description of its creation. Otherwise, no description of the earth's creation is given. Thus, the account says that God first created the heavens and the earth, or at least the material from which he later gives them final form.

In order to interpret Genesis 1:1 properly, however, we must discover the meaning of two key words. The word *shamayim* ("heaven") is used in three senses in the Bible: (1) the unseen abode of God, which is presumably uncreated; (2) the place where the stars are (outer space); and (3) the place where the birds fly (the air or atmosphere).[4] In Genesis 1:1, the word is apparently used in the second or third sense, or possibly more broadly to encompass both.

The word *eretz* ("earth") is also used in several ways, including: (1) the whole world (planet Earth), (2) the dry land, and (3) a country or region.[5] The first sense is probably intended here, as seas are not yet mentioned and the scope of the account makes the third usage too limited.

We suggest that Genesis 1:1 refers to the creation of the material which is to make up heaven and earth, whether the whole universe or merely the planet is in view. The following verses then describe God's activity in forming this material into various finished products, where the planet Earth, rather than the whole cosmos, receives almost all of the attention.

Ancient Hebrew, it is generally agreed, is far less abstract than ancient Greek or modern English.[6] Accordingly, we suggest that Genesis 1 gives a description of what the various creation events would have looked like to an earthbound observer had one been present to see God's work. This is not intended, however, to displace the understanding that the account is also a revelation from the Creator.

Genesis 1:2

And the earth was formless and void, and darkness was over the surface of the deep; and the Spirit of God was moving over the surface of the waters. Both *tohu* ("formless") and *bohu* ("void") occur only rarely in the Bible, and their meaning is, therefore, difficult to pinpoint. But the translation given above (similar to the KJV) is certainly possible. The Hebrew lexicon of Brown, Driver and Briggs gives "formlessness, confusion, unreality, emptiness" for *tohu*,[7] and the smaller but more recent translation by Holladay of the Koehler and Baumgartner lexicon has "wasteland, nothingness, nonentity."[8] For *bohu,* BDB gives "emptiness,"[9] while Holladay lists "void, waste."[10]

Many interpreters see the earth as already a solid planet at this point in the narrative, so they translate *tohu* and *bohu* as "waste and empty," meaning that the planet has its present shape and size, but that its surface is not yet fit for living creatures. Some interpreters go further, and suggest that the planet had been devastated by the judgment of God in conjunction with the fall of Satan.

On the other hand, the Jews who translated the book of Genesis into Greek more than two centuries before the time of Christ rendered these two words by *aoratos* ("invisible") and *akataskeuastos* ("unprepared, unfurnished") respectively.[11] Although these translations may be periphrastic, the men who made them cannot be accused of attempting to harmonize Genesis with *modern* science!

In agreement with the Septuagint, the KJV and most modern translations, and within the range suggested by modern lexicographers, we suggest that the earth at this point in the narrative is not yet a solid body, but is shapeless and empty, perhaps even invisible. This is an excellent, though nontechnical description of the gas cloud that would eventually form the earth, as discussed in chapter 3.

The second clause of verse 2 suggests that the earth is

in darkness. Whether it has been dark from creation up to this time (the usual interpretation), or whether it became dark at some time after its creation, is not stated in the narrative. This would depend on whether the second clause adds further details to the description of the earth given in the first clause or, alternatively, narrates a further development. The context does not remove this ambiguity, but we suggest the latter—that the earth, a shapeless, empty cloud, becomes dark as contraction raises the density enough to block out starlight.

The words *tehom* ("deep") and *mayim* ("waters") in the third clause immediately suggest the sea. This is certainly a possible translation, which if true would imply that the planet is already formed and covered with water. This fits the model of those who would describe the earth at this point as "waste and uninhabited" rather than "shapeless and vacuous."

But although *tehom* is usually associated with the sea, this is not always the case. Ezekiel 31:4 speaks of a tree growing because of waters, but the "deep" mentioned is presumably in the earth rather than the sea. The blessings upon Joseph in Genesis 49:25 and Deuteronomy 33: 13 also seem to refer to moisture deep in the ground instead of ocean depths. Psalm 71:20 refers to resurrection from the grave as being brought up from the "depths of the earth," and there seems to be no connection with water here. The Septuagint version of Genesis 1:2 uses *abyssos* ("abyss, bottomless, unfathomable") for *tehom*. A good fit may be made with the scientific model proposed in chapter 4 if this is understood as a description of the gas cloud, now a dark, cloudy and unfathomable region of space.

Likewise the word *mayim*, which is nearly always translated "water" or "waters," has a broader meaning than one might at first suppose. It is occasionally used for other fluids (or at least mixtures involving more than water (for example, urine, 2 Kings 18:27; semen, Is. 48:1). Also, it is used in reference to the solid and vapor states of H_2O (ice: Job 37:10; 38:30; vapor or droplets: 2 Sam. 22:5; Job 26:8; 36:27-28; Jer. 51:16).

The exact meaning of *mayim* in Genesis 1:2 is therefore uncertain, but a large body of ice or water, a mass of ice crystals or droplets, a large cloud of water vapor, or even some other fluid altogether would be within range of the usage of the word throughout Scripture. All of these would have a surface over which the Spirit of God might "move" or "hover." In agreement with the scientific model proposed, a dark nebula would be expected to contain some water vapor.[12]

An alternative possibility is that *mayim* is intended to intimate something of the chemical, rather than the physical, composition of the cloud: Water consists of hydrogen and oxygen, and the cloud consists principally of *hydrogen*, helium, carbon, nitrogen and *oxygen*. *Mayim* is one of the few Hebrew words which could communicate such information.

Some have translated "Spirit of God" here as "wind of God" or even "mighty wind," so that some natural or supernatural movement of the "deep" might be pictured. This is certainly possible, but the very frequent use of this phrase for the Holy Spirit, as well as the continual action of God throughout the creation account, supports the traditional interpretation.

Genesis 1:3-4

Now, after the darkness, comes light: *Then God said, "Let there be light"; and there was light. And God saw that the light was good; and God separated the light from the darkness.* This is certainly in agreement with the scientific model proposed above, in which the contracting gas cloud, having become dark within, eventually heats up to the point that it begins to glow.

But this is a strange sort of light, for we are explicitly told that God (later?) separates it from the darkness. Taking these clauses to be ordered chronological developments (rather than further description of a static situation), it would appear that our hypothetical observer first sees darkness everywhere, then light everywhere, then some of both after they are separated.

From the viewpoint of an observer riding along with the material of the earth as it is being formed, this is just what our scientific model would predict. When the gas cloud first begins to contract, the observer can see stars outside (not mentioned in Genesis). Later the contraction becomes sufficient to absorb light from outside the cloud, and the observer within is in the dark ("darkness was over the surface of the deep"). After further contraction and heating, however, the whole cloud lights up and the observer, immersed in light, can see no darkness anywhere ("and there was light"). Then, when the observer follows the equatorial band of gas and dust out from inside the cloud, both darkness and light are simultaneously visible.

Genesis 1:5

And God called the light day, and the darkness He called night. And there was evening and there was morning, one day. Darkness has been mentioned previously, but it is only now called "night"; the same is true for "light" and "day." But just as we ordinarily do not call the darkness of a cave "night" nor the light of a lamp "day," it appears that this is the beginning of night and day as ordinarily understood. Now it is just at this time in our scientific model, when the planet Earth condenses out of the equatorial dust and is rotating on its axis (see pp. 46-51), that it is proper to identify light with "day" and darkness with "night." That is, the illuminated side of a planet is experiencing day and the darkened side, night. We suggest, then, that the planet Earth becomes a solid body at this point in the Genesis account and not before.

The second sentence of this verse and the parallel passages which come later in Genesis 1 have traditionally been understood to teach that the events of creation took place in six consecutive, twenty-four-hour days. Our earlier discussion of *yom* ("day") indicated that it is commonly, though not universally, used to specify a period of daylight (about 12 hours) or a day-night pair (24 hours). Likewise the words *ereb* ("evening") and *boker* ("morning") are only rarely used in any other sense than as part of a normal day. The exceptions to the usual meanings of these words (for example, "day" in Gen. 2:4 for the whole creative period; "day of the Lord" in many places; "morning and evening" in Ps. 90:6, possibly referring to the life cycle of grass) make it possible to suggest that the days of creation were long but strictly bounded periods of time, for which no more suitable Hebrew word is available. Still, other things being equal, the most common meanings of the words involved should be used in constructing a model.

In this regard, it is interesting to note that Genesis 1 does not say that the activity described in verses 1-5a occurred on the first day, nor that those of verses 6-8a occurred on the second day, and likewise for days three through six. The traditional understanding of the passage is that all the events preceding a particular day occurred on that day, but tradition should be no more than suggestive in seeking a proper interpretation of the Bible.

I suggest that the "days" of Genesis 1 are twenty-four-hour days, sequential but not consecutive, and that the creative activity largely occurs between days rather than on them. That is, each Genesis day introduces a new creative period. (See figure 5 which illustrates this suggestion. The objection based on Ex. 20:11 was discussed in chapter 4.)

Genesis 1:6-8

Then God said, "Let there be an expanse in the midst of the waters, and let it separate the waters from the waters." And God made the expanse, and separated the waters which were below the expanse from the waters which were above the expanse; and it was so. And God called the expanse heaven. And there was evening and there was morning, a second day. The word *raqiah*, here translated "expanse" (KJV: "firmament"), means something spread out. It is most commonly used for the object created here in the Genesis narrative. Most scholars associate it with the sky, but some see it as a huge dome and others as the atmosphere. It appears to us that the firmament is the atmosphere for several reasons. (1) Nothing is said of any space between the firmament and the lower waters, nor of the firmament moving to separate the waters, so the firmament seems to fill the space between the upper and lower waters. (2) The birds are said to fly "upon the face" of the firmament (Gen. 1:20, literal Hebrew). The preposition *al* used here means "upon" not "below," suggesting that the birds are flying upon the air rather than beneath a dome. (3) The Hebrews were well aware that the air supported water in the form of clouds, and the phrase "waters which were above the expanse" is actually broad enough in the Hebrew to describe clouds floating in the sky.[13]

Given this understanding of the expanse or firmament, the Genesis account then describes the formation of the atmosphere after the earth has become a solid body. The presence of water is indicated in the text, so the sea is already present, or it is formed simultaneously with the atmosphere.

As noted earlier, many interpreters would put the origin of the earth as a solid body back at Genesis 1:2 or before, understanding the "waters" in verse 2 to be the sea. On the other hand, we suggested that the earth was not a solid object at that time and understood the "waters" to be the gas cloud from which the proto-earth was forming. Job 38:8-9 seems to speak of the origin of the seas, an event not explicitly mentioned in Genesis 1:

Or who enclosed the sea with doors,
When, bursting forth, it went out from the womb;
When I made a cloud its garment,
And thick darkness its swaddling band. . . .

The following verses in Job 38 also connect this event with confining the seas in designated locations, which seems to be the subject of Genesis 1:9-10, immediately following the passage we are now considering. Naturally, then, the sea is in existence no later than Genesis 1:8. But how much earlier was it in existence? Not earlier than the solid earth, according to Job, although liberal Old Testament scholars have usually connected the Genesis account with the Babylonian *Enuma Elish* creation account which starts with water. That Job calls the clouds the garment which God put around the sea when it was born suggests that the clouds (and therefore the atmosphere) were present when the sea was formed. To reconcile Job and Genesis, we suggest that the sea "burst forth" from its "womb," the earth, at the same time that the atmosphere was forming by outgassing from the earth's interior, which just happens to be in agreement with modern geophysical understanding.

Therefore, as the second day opens another period of creative activity, the solid earth is now completely covered with water and with an atmosphere of some sort involving a thick cloud cover.

Genesis 1:9-10

Then God said, "Let the waters below the heavens be gathered into one place, and let the dry land appear"; and it was so. And God called the dry land earth, and the gathering of the waters He called seas; and God saw that it was good. The Genesis account seems to teach quite clearly that the earth was once totally covered with water, after which time dry land appeared. Indeed, there is certainly enough water on earth to cover the entire globe if the earth once had no differences in elevation greater than two miles.

As discussed in chapter 3, the present crust of the earth consists of two rather different types, one corresponding to the continents and the other to the ocean bottoms. The continental-type crust is relatively thick, on the order of 25 to 30 miles, but relatively light, consisting of minerals whose composition is dominated by silicon and aluminum. The ocean bottom crust, on the other hand, is much thinner, usually only 4 to 6 miles thick, but it is composed of a relatively heavier mixture of minerals, compounded from elements dominated by silicon and magnesium. Because the lighter continental crust "floats" on the ocean bottom crust, a much greater range of heights and depths on the earth's surface is produced than would otherwise be the case. Therefore, if the crust at one time in earth's history were all of one sort, whether continental or ocean bottom type, the difference between highest and lowest levels very likely would have been small enough for a universal ocean.

There are at least two possible explanations for the present structure of the surface crust. If the original surface had been the crust of the continental type, the recently discovered movement of different parts of the earth's surface (the so-called continental drift) would have opened cracks in some places, which would have been filled at a lower level by the heavier silicon-magnesium crust, gradually producing basins into which the ocean water would run off. Meanwhile the collision of the continental crust at other locations would produce mountains and pile up the lighter crust so that it would no longer cover the whole planet nor be covered by the oceans.

Alternatively, if the original surface (beneath the universal ocean) was once like the present sub-oceanic crust, then volcanic activity would have produced islands and small continents of the heavy silicon-magnesium crust. Erosion and deposition would gradually produce sediments forming the lighter silicon-aluminum crust, the magnesium being removed by solution in the water, leaving the less soluble aluminum to dominate. At present, this latter alternative seems to fit our geophysical knowledge better.

Some Christians have thought the Genesis account suggests a single continent at this point, because it speaks of the waters being gathered into one place, which, on the surface of a sphere, permits only one continent. (This would fit the geologists' picture of the continent Pangea, which later broke up into Laurasia and Gondwanaland. The current data, however, is not yet sufficient to support such a conclusion. The geological evidence for a single continent goes back only a few hundred million years, which is probably long after the original dry land appeared. Much more geological research is necessary in order to determine the situation that existed when dry land first appeared from the ocean.) Proper interpretation of Scripture does not require us to treat the phrase "one place" as though an observer looking at the globe would see only one ocean as the land emerged. This seems to be refuted in the context by the use of the plural *yamin* ("seas") instead of the singular *yam*. Instead, we should understand "one place" as one *kind* of place, namely ocean basins.

Genesis 1:11-13

Then God said, "Let the earth sprout vegetation, plants yielding seed, and fruit trees bearing fruit after their kind, with seed in them, on the earth"; and it was so. And the earth brought forth vegetation, plants yielding seed after their kind, and trees bearing fruit, with seed in them, after their kind; and God saw that it was good. And there was evening and there was morning, a third day.

With the appearance of dry land, the Genesis account first mentions life. This is not to say that there was no life on earth before this time, but perhaps only that our hypothetical human observer would now, for the first time, begin to see life of a size and type for which there were words in ancient Hebrew.

Following the scheme previously suggested for the days

of Genesis 1—twenty-four-hour days which introduce new creative periods—it is not necessary to suppose that the fruit trees of this passage were created before any kind of animal life, which would contradict the fossil record understood as a chronological sequence. Instead, we assume that the creative period involving land vegetation began before the creative periods involving sea, air and land animals of sorts big enough to be noticed by an average human observer. In any case, since vegetation is only mentioned once in the whole Genesis account, it is possible that all vegetation is mentioned together merely for economy of expression, or to indicate its significance as the foundation upon which animal life builds. A recent evolutionary film follows this pattern,[14] although it can hardly be urged that evolutionists believe all vegetation developed before most of the animals.

Without further revelation, it is not possible to say for certain why God chose to introduce the plants at this point in the narrative, but it is undeniably logical for the appearance of land to precede land vegetation! Also, since the Genesis account seems to be aimed at man as the climax of God's creation, the account naturally proceeds from the creation of man's non-living environment to his vegetable and then animal environment. The only real exception to this logical order occurs during the creative period opened by the third day. Genesis 1:14-19 narrates what seems to be one of the most significant and striking details of the whole Genesis account.

Genesis 1:14-19

Then God said, "Let there be lights in the expanse of the heavens to separate the day from the night, and let them be for signs, and for seasons, and for days and years; and let them be for lights in the expanse of the heavens to give light on the earth"; and it was so. And God made the two great lights, the greater light to govern the day, and the lesser light to govern the night; He made the stars also. And

God placed them in the expanse of the heavens to give light on the earth, and to govern the day and the night, and to separate the light from the darkness; and God saw that it was good. And there was evening and there was morning, a fourth day.

Traditionally, it has been held that the sun and moon did not exist until this point in the creation account. Such a view is still maintained by those who feel that the whole universe was created in six consecutive twenty-four-hour days a few thousand years ago. However, in the light of our modern knowledge that the day-night sequence is caused by sunlight and the earth's rotation, it seems gratuitous to suppose that God here substitutes the sun for some other *unspecified* source of light (previously created in Gen. 1:3) without any statement given to this effect. Since the Genesis account has already mentioned atmospheric water, and since Job 38:9 speaks of clouds and "thick darkness" covering the seas, it is more reasonable to suppose that Genesis 1:14-19 describes the first appearance of the sun, moon and stars to our hypothetical earthbound observer on the occasion of the breakup of the earth's cloud cover.

It is worth noting that the Genesis account emphasizes the purpose of these heavenly bodies—to appear as lights in the sky, to mark off seasons, days and years—and in particular for the sun and moon to dominate the day and night, respectively. These purposes could not be accomplished if the sky were continually covered by clouds, even if the clouds were thin enough for diffuse sunlight to produce a definite period of daylight. For until the clouds had cleared enough to expose the sun, the observer would not be able to see what was producing the day-night sequence.

If this is the proper understanding of Genesis 1:14-19, then the sequence of the Genesis account is striking indeed. The author has delayed one important aspect of the physical environment—the final clearing and preparation of the atmosphere in its present breathable form—until after he has mentioned the plants. This appears at first to be an illogical "wrinkle" in the otherwise ordered sequence of the Genesis account. But according to many planetologists (see p. 52), vegetation was the immediate cause of both the oxygenation of the atmosphere and the removal of the cloud cover. Hence, there is no "wrinkle" and the appearance of vegetation in the narrative prior to the appearance of the sun, moon and stars is quite natural.

6

Creation Days and Creative Periods

The suggested synthesis of the scientific model proposed in chapter 3 and the biblical account has been explained throughout the exegesis of Genesis 1 in chapter 5. It remains only to summarize and clarify the basic points.

Summary

I suggest that the creation events described in Genesis took place over a long period of time. Indeed, they are still going on (see figure 6).

The long, horizontal bars in figure 6 are creative periods as in a day-age model with overlapping days. Unlike such a view, however, these periods are not identified with the days of Genesis 1, which are represented by narrow vertical bars. The creative periods overlap. Although they begin in sequence, they end together at the seventh day (still future) when God will have completed his creation. Thus the planet Earth began to be formed when God created the universe 15 billion to 20 billion years ago. Its formation was essentially completed about 4½ billion years ago, when day one introduces the formation of earth's atmosphere and ocean.

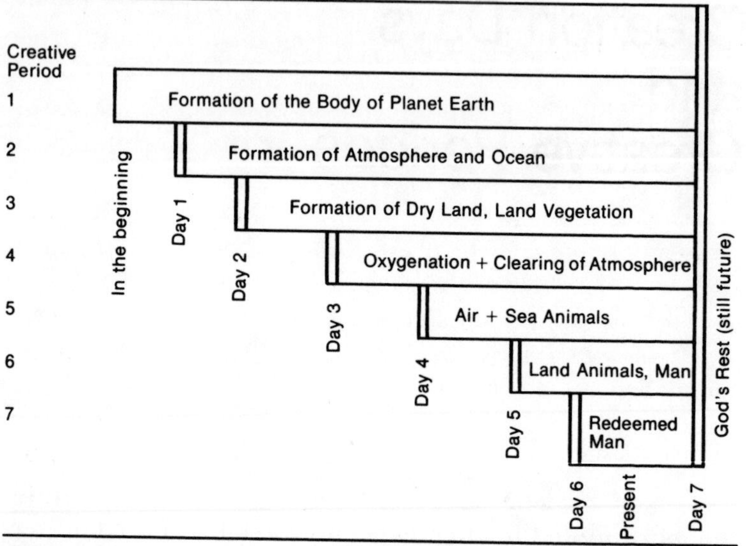

Figure 6: Synopsis of creative activity according to proposed Modified Intermittent-Day View

Yet accretion of matter to the body of the planet continues even today with the infall of meteoritic material. Likewise God's major activity in forming the atmosphere and ocean occurred long ago, but volcanoes still bring smaller amounts of gases and water to the surface. Similarly, the continental or plate drift, which we suggested brought about the appearance of dry land, is still shifting the pieces around and occasionally producing more dry land in the process, though its major work in creation is over.

Land vegetation was created long ago, yet God built into it an adaptability to meet changing environments. The original clearing of the atmosphere occurred after the appearance of large quantities of vegetation, yet vegetation continues to protect animal life from asphyxiation by preventing the accumulation of CO_2. This in turn prevents a planetary "heat death" (as on Venus) by moderating the earth's greenhouse effect. As with the plants, we suggest that man and the animals have long been created in their original kinds, yet they continue to demonstrate their built-in adaptability to changing conditions by a sort of descent with modification as, for example, in the development of bacteria resistant to antibiotics.

The most unusual feature of this model is that day seven is in the future and the present age is characterized as principally concerned with the creation of redeemed man (that is, the redemption of fallen man). As pointed out in chapter 4, Hebrews 4:1-11 seems to indicate that God's sabbath rest described in Genesis 2:2 was either present or future in the first century A.D. In John 5:17, Jesus seems to be saying that God was still creating at that time, so the sabbath rest would appear to be future. Keeping in mind that the idea of redemption involves rescue, and implies the fall of man, this view of creation is quite different from the straight-line improvement process as seen by some theistic evolutionists. I suggest that the redemption of creation from the bondage to which God subjected it (Rom. 8:18-25) and the appearance of the new heavens and the new earth (Rev. 21:1-8) mark the seventh day and the beginning of God's rest.

But what is the significance of these peculiar literal days in our proposed model of the Genesis account? After all, even though each day introduces a new creative period, only the seventh marks the complete cessation of creative activity in the previous periods. My suggestion is that God highlights these seven days, among the many actually occurring during creation, in order to set up an ordinance by which man is to commemorate creation. The six days of work remind him that he was created by God, and the seventh day of rest looks forward to God's rest, when redeemed man will rejoice with all creation in the new heavens and new earth (Rom. 8:18-25; Heb. 4:1-11).

This highlighting of one feature in a context is seen also in other covenantal enactments of God. The rainbow, for example, is taken from among the events following the flood as a sign of God's covenant with Noah (Gen. 9:13). Bread and wine are taken from a Passover supper (Mk. 14: 12, 22-24) as a sign of Christ's covenant with believers. In each case (the rainbow, bread and wine, and the seven days of the week) the sign looks both backward (to the flood, Gen. 9:11; to Christ's death, Mk. 14:22-24; to the creation, Ex. 20:11) and forward (no future destruction by water, Gen. 9:15; Christ's coming kingdom, Mk. 14:25; the new heavens and earth, Heb. 4:1-11).

Turning from chronology to other details in the creation account, table 4 indicates the principal correlations between the biblical materials and scientific theory.

Conclusion

In this work we have made some unusual suggestions for the understanding of the origin and early history of the earth. It is not to be expected that these suggestions are the "last word" for investigation even in this particular area of the relationship between science and Scripture. With millions of people again speaking (modern) Hebrew as their native language, a much stronger foundation now exists for the study of that ancient Hebrew in which the Old Testament was written. Further aid is to be expected as archaeology continues to uncover and assimilate materials written in Hebrew or other ancient cognate languages.

From the side of science, we are still in the opening years of the space age. As yet we have detailed information from the surface of only two planets, Earth and Mars, and one natural satellite, our moon. It may be expected that further instrumented landings on Venus and Mars and artificial satellites in orbit around Jupiter and Saturn will add substantially in the coming years to the data available for the construction of theories on the origin of the earth and solar system.

For those already convinced of the reliability of Scripture as a revelation from God, these times will provide exciting opportunities to serve the Lord in vindicating his Word to those who need it but are afraid to trust it. Careful research in the area of science/Scripture interactions may be expect-

A Correlation of Biblical Material and Scientific Theory on the Origin of the Earth

Biblical Material (see chap. 5)	**Scientific Theory (see chap. 3)**
In the beginning God created heaven and earth (Gen. 1:1)	A beginning—the "big bang," perhaps
Earth without form, void (Gen. 1:2)	Earth an amorphous, tenuous nebula
Darkness on face of deep (Gen. 1:2)	After some contraction, cloud becomes opaque, dark within
Spirit of God moves on face of waters (Gen. 1:2)	(Providential oversight and occasional intervention)
Let there be light (Gen. 1:3)	Further contraction causes cloud to glow
Light divided from darkness (Gen. 1:4)	Planetary material thrust outside glowing cloud
Light = day, darkness = night (Gen. 1:5)	Planet condenses from planetesimals; sun and rotation give day-night sequence
First day intervenes (Gen. 1:5)	
Waters burst forth from womb of earth (Job 38:8-9); firmament appears in midst of waters (Gen. 1:6)	Earth is heated within by pressure and radioactivity, driving out water and gases to form atmosphere and ocean
Division of waters above and below firmament (Gen. 1:6-7)	Presence of atmosphere allows both surface and atmospheric water
Second day intervenes (Gen. 1:8)	
Gathering of waters, dry land appears (Gen. 1:9-10)	Continental material develops from sub-oceanic by means of vulcanism, erosion
Earth brings forth vegetation (Gen. 1:11-12)	Land vegetation appears
Third day intervenes (Gen. 1:13)	
Lights appear in the sky to mark off days, seasons, to dominate day (sun) and night (moon) (Gen. 1:14-18)	Photosynthesis by vegetation replaces CO_2 by oxygen, lowering temperature and clearing atmosphere so astronomical objects visible; also prepares atmosphere for animals and man
Fourth day intervenes (Gen. 1:19)	

Table 4

ed to be an important means to this end. It is hoped that this book will encourage Christians in believing that God has communicated basic (and even complex) scientific truths in the nontechnical vocabulary of ancient Israel, and that it is not necessary to *limit* the message of the first two chapters of Genesis to the statement "God is really behind it all, however it happened." On the other hand, we trust that other Christians may realize that scientific research can perform a real service, just as archaeology has, in helping us to re-examine and retest traditional exegeses of various biblical passages.

For those who feel that the scientific veracity of Scripture has been discredited since Galileo or Darwin, we hope this work will cause a sympathetic re-examination of orthodox Christianity, leading them to the biblical Jesus of history, who alone can meet our every need.

Appendix 1

Nonradiometric Data Relevant to the Question of Age[1]

Daniel E. Wonderly

Within the past twenty years several useful types of age-indicating data have become available. An abundance of objective research reports on these subjects can now be easily found in scientific journals and other publications. It is time for creationists to begin to make far more use of such reports than we have in the past. We have often failed to realize that these are very helpful in making estimates of the earth's age. The record of God's work in nature is far more complete, informative and worthy of consideration than creationists have usually thought.

It is our purpose here to list some of the specific types of data available, giving a few selected bibliographic references for each type. These sources have been carefully chosen with a view to their being sufficient to serve as at least a "starter" for anyone wishing to pursue a given subject. Most of the sources themselves also have good bibliographies, which will readily enable any interested person to locate numerous additional articles on the subject. An effort has been made to choose those articles and monographs which consist primarily of the objective results of research rather than of theory. However, in the references in which evolutionary theory may appear the presence of some theoretical material need not obscure the facts which were obtained in the research. The reader should keep in mind, for example, that long periods of time do not necessarily imply evolutionary development. All of the types of data which are listed below appear to be in keeping with the historical account of creation found in Genesis 1 and 2.

Most of the bibliographic entries are available at the geology library of practically any large university. Other materials can be obtained from the geological societies of major oil-producing states and by means of interlibrary loans. The addresses of most of the geological societies can be found in the Directory near the back of each issue of the *American Association of Petroleum Geologists Bulletin*. Many of the sources can be used and understood without an extensive background in geology. This paper is basically a *listing* of types of data, rather than a composite monograph. [The numbers at the end of each section of this appendix are not footnotes. They refer to the corresponding sections in the bibliography (pp. 144-50). Ed.] Thus the reader will be able to consider any one subject separately and locate the bibliographic references for that subject easily.

Highly Organized Carbonate Deposits

Drilling records from the sedimentary carbonate deposits of the Great Bahama Bank, off the coast of Florida, indicate a multilayered deposit of various forms of limestone and dolomite somewhat in excess of 14,500 feet in thickness. In the deeper parts, dolomites alternate with limestones, with evidence of erosion between four major cycles of deposition. Identifiable fossils were found to a depth of at least 10,600 feet. Alternations between limestone and dolomites in this and similar formations indicate at least a corresponding number of changes of environment during deposition and during the process of dolomite formation. (See below on dolomite formation and limestone formation.) Also, the unconformities, at the levels where erosion is revealed, must represent significant amounts of time.[1]

Ooids Formed Gradually

The distribution and rates of formation of the small, spheroidal bodies known as ooids, oolites (more properly refers to rocks containing the individual ooids) or ooliths yield evidence of the earth's age. Most ooids are concentrically laminated around a core of extraneous material such as a grain of sand, a small shell fragment or a recrystallized fecal pellet. This process of adding concentric layers (which can be readily observed with a microscope) is accomplished by a slow accretion of mineral which is extracted from the sea water on the beach where the ooids are being formed. The present-day formation of carbonate ooids is observable on numerous shores where shallow water carbonate deposition is taking place. Oolitic limestone, with ooids of various types, appears at numerous levels in the Great Bahama Bank and in many other carbonate deposits.[2]

Modern Sediments Compared to Ancient

The similarities between the order of deposition of present-day marine sediments and the order found in deep subsurface sedimentary deposits in oil fields are now being used by oil research geologists for understanding and predicting the arrangement of older deposits deep in the earth. The research also deals with paleoecological topics, such as the faunal associations and ecological succession found in ancient strata, comparing them to modern faunal associations observed in shallow-water depositional environments. Even though we cannot accept all the tenets of uniformitarianism, the close similarities between modern marine carbonate deposition and these ancient deposits demand that we recognize slow, natural deposition as accounting for many thick carbonate deposits in the oil fields.[3]

Oceanic Sedimentation

Oceanic sedimentation refers to the thickness and arrangement of the layers of carbonate and siliceous skeletal remains found on the ocean floor, formed by the accumulation of the shells of Foraminifera, Radiolaria and other planktonic organisms. A comparison of the thickness of such deposits with current rates of deposition of these skeletons in parts of the ocean floor where there is no evidence of rapid deposition or recent disturbance is meaningful. Of special significance are the pelagic sediments found in isolated parts of the ocean, such as the tops of certain seamounts and abyssal hills. These are far enough from land masses that the rate of deposition is not appreciably affected by currents bringing sediments from those land masses.[4]

Fossilization Still Occurring

It has sometimes been said that the processes of fossilization are not occurring today, but recent studies have revealed numerous cases of the current burial and fossilization of calcareous plant and invertebrate animal skeletons in marine coastal environments, on the sea floor and in the subsurface of modern reefs.[5]

Dolomite Formation

The rate of dolomite formation in modern marine environments has been usefully compared to a study of ancient formations which exhibit alternating dolomite (dolostone) and calcium carbonate (limestone) strata. In recent years the process of natural dolomite production has been observed and studied in several marine environments which have the proper conditions for the necessary magnesium ions to be extracted from the sea water and deposited. There are many lines of very strong evidence indicating that practically all dolomites—both ancient and modern—are formed by a process of replacement of calcium carbonate particles in lime sediment or limerock. In order for dolomitization of such a sediment or rock to occur there must be a ratio of Mg and Ca ions in the water which will favor the formation of dolomite, and there must be extensive circulation of the water over the sediment or through pores in the rock. Because dolomitization proceeds by ion exchange, it is of necessity a slow process and cannot occur to any appreciable degree without extensive circulation of water.[6]

Deposits of Evaporites

Multilayered deposits of the (water soluble) evaporites anhydrite and salt often alternate not only with each other, but also with (relatively insoluble) calcium carbonate layers. The Castile Formation of west Texas and southeastern New Mexico is one such deposit. Its thickness is in excess of 2,000 feet in some places, and includes approximately 200,000 calcium carbonate-anyhdrite "couplet" layers. The nature of these thin layers of anhydrite and of calcium carbonate definitely shows that they were deposited by precipitation. It should be remembered that these two substances do not precipitate at the same degree of concentration of the sea water. Calcium carbonate begins to precipitate when the sea water has been evaporated to about half the original volume, but the precipitation of anhydrite does not begin until a volume of about 19% has been reached.

Thus it is evident that a major change in the concentration of the sea water took place 200,000 times, the concentration returning each time to at least very near the same value. Furthermore, each of the precipitation events had to be accompanied by quiet water to allow the mineral to settle to the bottom and form a thin, uniform layer. (The areal extent of these layers is many miles, with almost uniform thickness of any given layer maintained over at least a distance of 18 miles.) These are processes which required very considerable amounts of time.

Another very significant evaporite formation which shows conclusive evidence that it was formed slowly is that found in the Mediterranean Sea. In several areas core drillings beneath the sea floor have revealed repeating layers of fossil-bearing oceanic sediments interbedded with evaporite layers. This shows that the Mediterranean Sea has had a long history encompassing several extended periods of very low water and desert-like evaporative conditions, alternating with periods of normal marine deposition of sediments. Since neither the evaporative nor the normal marine sediments are of the types which could have been deposited by rapidly moving water, or in the aftermath of a flood, we are forced to recognize that the deposition time for this alternating series of sediments extended over several millions of years. Also in the Balearic abyssal plain, west of Corsica and Sardinia, a "bulls-eye pattern" of evaporite deposition was found. In this deposit, layers of $CaCo_3$, $CaSO_4$ and NaCl were found *in the normal order* of precipitation when evaporation of sea water occurs. There is good evidence that this evaporite deposit is a few thousand feet in thickness.[7]

Deposits of Sandstone and Shale

An example of multilayered deposits of sandstone and shale is found in the Haymond Formation in the Marathon region of Texas. There are approximately 15,000 thin sandstone layers alternating with approximately the same number of contrasting shale layers in this formation. The study of such a deposit requires that we carefully consider the length of time required for the clay particles, which formed each layer of shale, to settle out of suspension. The clay particles which form uniform layers such as this are extremely small. Thus they settle slowly and only when a minimum of turbulence exists.[8]

Modern Coral Reefs

The thicknesses of modern coral reefs, when related to the growth rates of reef-forming organisms, imply an old earth. The thickest deposit of this kind measured to date is that of the Eniwetok atoll, where the test drill penetrated 4,610 feet of coral deposit before reaching the volcanic seamount on which the reef was built. A study of such deposits in the light of present-day coral growth rates cannot produce an exact chronology of the past, but will nevertheless be very meaningful. This is so because of our recognition of the stability of God's natural laws, including the laws of nutrition, respiration and secretion in living organisms. According to detailed and extensive studies by A. G. Mayor (1924) on the growth rates of various genera of corals in the Samoan Islands (a tropical area where conditions are most favorable for rapid growth), the maximum rate of upward growth of the reef surfaces was only about 8 mm per year.[9]

Ancient Coral Reefs

In the oil fields of Canada there are ancient coral reefs or atolls which are frequently covered with extensive deposits of evaporites and other minerals. This is a geographic area where the process of comparing modern reefs and other modern carbonate deposits with the ancient has yielded spectacular results in predicting the best drilling sites (cf. reference 3). Some of the atoll reefs in the Rainbow Lake area of Alberta, Canada are 800 feet thick at the rim, and are strikingly similar to the crescent-atolls of the present-day Great Barrier Reef of Australia. The Rainbow Lake reefs contain abundant massive growths of colonial corals *in situ* (growth position), as well as crinoids, stromatoporoids, brachipods and gastropods. Thus, these were genuine, wave-resistant reefs which grew in ancient times when most of central North America was covered by relatively shallow ocean waters. The multiple layers of evaporites and other thick mineral deposits covering these reefs witness to the long periods of time which have elapsed since that geological period (the Devonian).[10]

Coral Growth Bands

Growth bands, exhibited by ancient and modern corals and mollusks, appear to be an accurate indicator of the daily growth rates of these organisms, as well as of the number of days in the year at the time when the animal was living. It has been known since the beginning of this century that the corallites of some kinds of modern corals possess annual growth bands. Within the last decade it has been learned that these corals possess two lesser orders of growth bands or ridges between the annual rings, one marking the growth increments of synodical lunar months, the other the increments of daily growth. When certain fossil corals from the deeper strata, e.g., from Devonian rocks of New York and Ontario, are examined, they are found to show growth bands very similar to those of modern corals, except that the number of daily bands between annual bands is approximately 400 instead of 365. This apparently indicates that these corals lived at a time when there were 400 days in the year, and consequently slightly less than 22 hours in the day. (The calculations of astronomers have shown clearly that the rate of rotation of the earth is decreasing, but that the period of the earth's revolution around the sun has been essentially constant. Thus, in earlier times, though the absolute length of the year was the same as now, the earth's rotation was more rapid, making the day shorter and also affecting the number of lunar—and tidal—months in a year.) The growth rings on the Devonian corals thus show that they lived and grew at a very early date; and the size of the rings shows that the growth rates of these corals were not very different from the growth rates of modern corals. The growth bands which have been observed on certain ancient bivalve mollusk shells are in essential agreement with the findings in corals.[11]

Organic Banks

Various types of ancient carbonate organic banks and cyclic deposits include layers of definite, identifiable fossils. The larger of these banks are usually spoken of as reefs in geologic literature. Examples are the famous "Horseshoe atoll" (or Scurry reef) of west Texas, the numerous Silurian reefs of Indiana, and the Capitan reef of west Texas and New Mexico. Organic banks which are moundlike in shape and enclosed in rock of a contrasting type are usually called bioherms, though the terms reef and bioherm are often applicable to the same structure.

Some of these organic banks are very large, lie at great depths and are components of extensive local stratigraphic columns. For example, the Capitan reef is 350 miles long, and 2,000 feet thick in places; its eastern half lies in a large oil field at a depth of some thousands of feet. Numerous alternating layers (cyclic deposits) of evaporites make up an extensive part of the formations which cover it. This reef has numerous bryozoan colonies and other fossils still in growth position (*in situ*). Beneath the Capitan reef there are, in some localities, more than 15,000 feet of sedimentary rock. This rock consists of numerous distinct layers of limestone, dolomite, sandstone, shale, etc., alternating with each other. Most of these deep layers underlying the reef possess identifiable fossils.

Often an organic bank will be associated with, or a part of, a group of repeating depositional units called cyclothems. A cyclothem is a series of sedimentary layers which repeats itself in the stratigraphic record in a particular locality. Each cyclothem represents the depositional results of a series of changing environments in the ancient locality involved. The fact that several very similar cyclothems sometimes exist in a local stratigraphic column, and that evaporite layers and other environmental indicators frequently make up a part of each cyclothem is conclusive evidence that these are naturally formed series representing rather large units of time. It is also significant that some cyclothems contain subcycles.

Calcareous algal limestone banks and mounds are often found lying deep in the strata of oil fields. These are, of course, a type of organic bank, having been produced by calcium-secreting algae which are similar to the many species of calcareous algae which we have today. The fossilized remains of the algae in these banks give every evidence of being *in situ*, and of having accumulated in a manner similar to the formation of algal deposits in modern tropical marine environments.

Recent extensive research has shed much light on the true nature of limestones such as those found in the organic banks. The study of the various types of organic banks together with a comparison of the carbonate depositional processes in modern marine environments has shown that a very high percentage of the limestone deposits of the earth was formed by the gradual accumulation of calcareous animals and plants, rather than by inorganic processes. Even though diagenetic change obliterates many of the skeletons of these organisms, sufficient parts usually remain (with some of the substrate material on which they were growing) so that we can be sure, at least in many cases, that they were preserved either at or near the place where they grew. Since most limerocks have large amounts of microscopically identifiable particles, it has been observed that the layers of major limestone deposits are usually composed of normal assemblages of grains and other characteristic particles. These are frequently very similar to the assemblages found in modern carbonate rock-forming environments such as those of the Caribbean area and other parts of the world.

Often the fossils found so abundantly in a given bed of limestone make up a typical marine faunal and floral community, and a significant percentage of the delicately articulated skeletons will be intact, showing that they were not transported any long distance. Also, the lack of signs of abrasion of certain carbonate grains, such as fecal pellets, in the rock, and the lack of size-sorting of the various types of grains are further evidence that the limestone was formed *in situ* without extensive transport of the materials of which it is composed. One of the most spectacular examples of evidence for the *in situ* formation of limestones as a result of the growth of organisms is the rounded, laminated masses of limestone which are called stromatolites. Extensive study of very similar structures being formed today in some carbonate depositional environments has made possible a detailed analysis of the ancient stromatolites. (Each stromatolite is formed by a large mass of algae growing in the water and collecting layers of carbonate grains on its gelatinous surface as the water sweeps over it.)

The presence of layers of shale between the layers of limestone in many formations has usually aided in the preservation of the skeletal material and in the identification of the environments in which the limestone layers were accumulated.[12]

Stratigraphic Columns

Well logs and drilling cores from oil fields provide us with the structure and composition of entire *local* stratigraphic columns. In the past we have too often neglected to study the deeper parts of the local stratigraphic columns in areas where we have focused attention upon a single geologic formation. There now are available in the literature of petroleum geology very complete records of the local columns in many geographic areas. For example, Hughes (1954) gives the 16,705-foot column of the Richardson and Bass No. 1 Harrison-Federal well, in the Delaware Basin of southeast New Mexico, as a 167-inch printed column. By devoting one inch to each 100 feet of well core he was able to show the lithology of the entire well in considerable detail. Also included are the generic names of some of the fossils, to a depth of 16,000 feet. Such records as this help make possible a study of both the chemical and physical nature of the contrasting layers in the column, as well as of some of the types of animals and plants present at the times of deposition. The availability of these well logs and drilling cores makes it possible for interested persons to study the geologic record directly, without having to depend on composite columns or abbreviated summaries.[13]

Distribution of Marine Fossils

Marine fossils are distributed unequally in limestone and other formations. An example of this is the abundance of certain kinds of very dense, thick-shelled mollusks of Class Pelecypoda in the upper strata, but the absence of the same types in lower layers. Conversely, some of the less dense animals, for example, numerous species of arthropods of Class Trilobita, are abundant in lower strata but are not found in upper layers. Recent electron microscope studies of the chitin of trilobite skeletons give evidence for a low density for these animals. Similarly, many species of the cephalopods, of Phylum Mollusca, though very buoyant due to the air chambers of their shells, are found only in the deeper strata of the earth, indicating that they were buried before the formation of the Mesozoic and Cenozoic strata and became extinct before those strata were laid down. Thus, the unequal distribution of marine fossils is another indication of the long history which these organisms have. The theory of some proponents of "flood geology" which says that the unequal distribution is largely due to densities is shown to be erroneous.

Even the very fact that many types of fossils are abundant in only a small per cent of the stratigraphic column in a given locality, but not found at all in other parts of that column, should be a cause for much serious study. In such columns a great many species which are present at the lower levels are not present in the upper strata at that site, nor in the corresponding upper strata at other sites. The prevalence of this condition calls for recognition of a long period of time for the formation of the larger (thicker and more extensive) stratigraphic columns.[14]

Forest Deposits

Data collected during the study made by Dorf and his associates of the multiple forest deposits in Yellowstone National Park apparently have not been used to any extent by creationist writers. Numerous types of fossil vegetation and preserved foliage were discovered in the strata of Specimen Ridge and Amethyst Mountain. Whitcomb and Morris have tried to explain these forest deposits by saying the trees were floated into place during the Flood, forming a semblance of successive forests preserved in volcanic ash. The work of Dorf makes this theory completely unacceptable.[15]

Sea-Floor Spreading

Present and past rates of sea-floor spreading are exhibited in the oceanic ridges and in the thickness of pelagic sediments which lie upon the ocean floor at various distances from the present midline of the ridges. The present rate of sea-floor spreading along the Mid-Atlantic ridge is estimated to be only a few centimeters per year. The fact that the sediments are thin near the center-line of the ridge and become thicker farther away from the ridge, on each side, is an indication that the spreading has been practically continuous for a long period of time. Also, the linear strips of igneous rock which lie to the west of the ridge are practically identical to the linear strips extending along the east side. Thus, one side forms a "mirror image" of the other with respect to the chemical and magnetic nature of the parallel trends of igneous rock. This gives us much reason to believe that each pair of corresponding strips was formed at approximately the same time, from the same mass of magma along the ridge, and that the slow spreading of the floor at the rift has resulted in their being widely separate now. The above-mentioned symmetry along the Mid-Atlantic ridge has been carefully mapped, and the two sides correspond for a distance of about 125 miles out from the center of the ridge.[16]

Magnetic Reversals

Geologic records indicate magnetic reversals in igneous bodies of rock (both on the continents and in the ocean floors) and in sediment cores taken from the ocean floor. A great many extensive rock masses exhibiting an orderly series of reversals have been discovered during the past ten years. For example, there is a close agreement between the series of reversals found in ancient lava flows of the Rocky Mountains and those in the Atlantic sea-floor. There are many strong evidences that most of the reversals which are "frozen" into the igneous rocks are separated from one another by at least hundreds of thousands of years.[17]

Potassium-Argon "Clock"

Even though we are here presenting a list of types of nonradiometric data, there is one phase of radiometric dating which should be mentioned because it has apparently gone unnoticed by a great many creationists.

The potassium-argon "clock," in rocks which effectively retain radiogenic Ar^{40}, is restarted whenever the rocks are heated (or reheated) to a temperature of 300° C. or more. Recent writers on this type of dating state that all original argon is lost when such heating of igneous and metamorphic rocks occurs. Thus when the amount of argon present is measured, only the amount produced in the rocks since they were last heated can be detected. This characteristic is often listed as a disadvantage, because this means that potassium-argon dates can give only the length of time since the rock mass was last cooled to a temperature below

300° C. However, this feature is an advantage for those who are interested in determining how long it has been since igneous or metamorphic rock masses were in a heated condition.

Perhaps we should also mention that Dalrymple, Moore and others recently discovered that some of the earlier potassium-argon dates obtained for igneous rocks which had been formed in deep water were very incorrect (much too old). Their research showed that whenever lava is erupted into a deep-water environment, the hydrostatic pressure and the rapid cooling caused by the cold water cause excess Ar^{40} to be "frozen" into the *outer parts* of the lava mass. Earlier, when this principle was not known, numerous samples of marine volcanic basalt were wrongly dated. However, now that the scientific world has been alerted to this principle, only the potassium-argon dates from continental formations and from samples taken from the interior of submarine masses of rock are considered reliable.[18]

Appendix 2

Primeval Chronology[1]

William Henry Green

The question of the possible reconciliation of the results of scientific inquiry respecting the antiquity of man and the age of the world with the Scripture chronology has been long and earnestly debated. On the one hand, scientists, deeming them irreconcilable, have been led to distrust the divine authority of the Scriptures; and, on the other hand, believers in the divine Word have been led to look upon the investigations of science with an unfriendly eye, as though they were antagonistic to religious faith. In my reply to Bishop Colenso in 1863, I had occasion to examine the method and structure of the biblical genealogies, and incidentally ventured the remark that herein lay the solution of the whole matter. I said:[2]

> There is an element of uncertainty in a computation of time which rests upon genealogies, as the sacred chronology so largely does. Who is to certify us that the antediluvian and ante-Abrahamic genealogies have not been condensed in the same manner as the post-Abrahamic?

> . . .Our current chronology is based upon the *prima facie* impression of these genealogies. . . . But, if these recently discovered indications of the antiquity of man, over which scientific circles are now so excited, shall, when carefully inspected and thoroughly weighed, demonstrate all that any have imagined they might demonstrate, what then? They will simply show that the popular chronology is based upon a wrong interpretation, and that a select and partial register of ante-Abrahamic names has been mistaken for a complete one.

Further reflection has confirmed me in the correctness of the opinion then expressed.

At the courteous request of the Editors of the *Bibliotheca Sacra* I here repeat, with a few verbal changes, the discussion of the biblical genealogies above referred to, and add some further considerations which seem to me to justify the belief that the genealogies in Genesis chapters 5 and 11 were not intended to be used, and cannot properly be used, for the construction of a chronology.

Genealogies Frequently Abbreviated

It can scarcely be necessary to adduce proof to one who has even a superficial acquaintance with the genealogies of the Bible, that these are frequently abbreviated by the omission of unimportant names. In fact, abridgment is the general rule induced by the indisposition of the sacred writers to encumber their pages with more names than were necessary for their immediate purpose. This is so constantly the case, and the reason for it so obvious, that the occurrence of it need create no surprise anywhere, and we are at liberty to suppose it whenever anything in the circumstances of the case favors that belief.

The omissions in the genealogy of our Lord as given in Matthew 1 are familiar to all. Thus in verse 8 three names are dropped between Joram and Ozias (Uzziah), namely, Ahaziah (2 Kings 8:25), Joash (2 Kings 12:1) and Amaziah

(2 Kings 14:1); and in verse 11 Jehoiakim is omitted after Josiah (2 Kings 23:34; 1 Chron. 3:16); and in verse 1 the entire genealogy is summed up in two steps, "Jesus Christ, the son of David, the son of Abraham."

Other instances abound elsewhere; we mention only a few of the most striking. In 1 Chronicles 26:24 we read in a list of appointments made by King David (see 1 Chron. 24:3; 25:1; 26:26), that Shebuel,[3] the son of Gershom, the son of Moses, was ruler of the treasures; and again in 1 Chronicles 23:15-16 we find it written, "The sons of Moses were Gershom and Eliezer. Of the sons of Gershom Shebuel was the chief." Now it is absurd to suppose that the author of Chronicles was so grossly ignorant as to suppose that the grandson of Moses could be living in the reign of David and appointed by him to a responsible office. Again in the same connection (1 Chron. 26:31), we read that "among the Hebronites was Jerijah the chief"; and this Jerijah, or Jeriah (for the names are identical), was, according to 23:19, the first of the sons of Hebron, and Hebron was (v. 12) the son of Kohath, the son of Levi (v. 6). So that if no contraction in the genealogical list is allowed, we have the great-grandson of Levi holding a prominent office in the reign of David.

The genealogy of Ezra is recorded in the book which bears his name; but we learn from another passage, in which the same line of descent is given, that it has been abridged by the omission of six consecutive names. This is made clear by the comparison on the next page.

Still further, Ezra relates (8:1, 2):

> These are now the chief of their fathers, and this is the genealogy of them that went up with me from Babylon, in the reign of Artaxerxes the king. Of the sons of Phinehas, Gershom. Of the sons of Ithamar, Daniel. Of the sons of David, Hattush.

Here, if no abridgment of the genealogy is allowed, we should have a great-grandson and a grandson of Aaron and a son of David coming up with Ezra from Babylon after the captivity.

1 Chronicles 6:3-14	*Ezra 7:1-5*	
1. Aaron	Aaron	
2. Eleazar	Eleazar	
3. Phinehas	Phinehas	
4. Abishua	Abishua	
5. Bukki	Bukki	
6. Uzzi	Uzzi	
7. Zerahiah	Zerahiah	
8. Meraioth	Meraioth	
9. Amariah		
10. Ahitub		six names
11. Zadok		omitted
12. Ahimaaz		by Ezra
13. Azariah		
14. Johanan		
15. Azariah	Azariah	
16. Amariah	Amariah	
17. Ahitub	Ahitub	
18. Zadok	Zadok	
19. Shallum	Shallum	
20. Hilkiah	Hilkiah	
21. Azariah	Azariah	
22. Seraiah	Seraiah	
	Ezra	

Different Relationships Classed Together

This disposition to abbreviate genealogies by the omission of whatever is unessential to the immediate purpose of the writer is shown by still more remarkable reductions than those which we have been considering. Persons of different degrees of relationship are sometimes thrown together under a common title descriptive of the majority and all words of explanation, even those which seem essential to the sense, are rigorously excluded, the supplying of these chasms being left to the independent knowledge of the reader. Hence several passages in the genealogies of Chronicles have now become hopelessly obscure. They may have been intelligible enough to contemporaries, but for those who have no extraneous sources of information the key to their explanation is wanting. In other cases we are able to understand them because the information necessary to make them intelligible is supplied from parallel passages of Scripture. Thus the opening verses of Chronicles contain the following bald list of names without a word of explanation: "Adam, Seth, Enosh, Kenan, Mahalalel, Jared, Enoch, Methuselah, Lamech, Noah, Shem, Ham, and Japheth."

We are not told who these persons are, how they were related to each other or whether they were related. The writer presumes that his readers have the book of Genesis in their hands and that the simple mention of these names in their order will be sufficient to remind them that the first ten names trace the line of descent from father to son from the first to the second great progenitor of mankind; and that the last three are brothers, although nothing is said to indicate that their relationship is different from the preceding.

Again the family of Eliphaz, the son of Esau, is spoken of in the following terms in 1 Chronicles 1:36: "The sons of Eliphaz: Teman and Omar, Zephi and Gatam, Kenaz and Timna, and Amalek."

Now by turning to Genesis 36:11-12 we shall see that the first five are sons of Eliphaz, and the sixth his concubine, who was the mother of the seventh. This is so plainly written in Genesis that the author of the Chronicles, were he the most inveterate blunderer, could not have mistaken it. But trusting to the knowledge of his readers to supply the omission, he leaves out the statement respecting Eliphaz's concubine, but at the same time connects her name and that of her son with the family to which they belong, and this though he was professedly giving a statement of the sons of Eliphaz.

So, likewise, in the pedigree of Samuel (or Shemuel, v. 33, the difference in orthography is due to our translators and is not in the original), which is given in 1 Chronicles 6 in both an ascending and descending series. Thus in verses 22-24: "The sons of Kohath; Amminadab his son, Korah his son, Assir his son, Elkanah his son, and Ebiasaph his son, and Assir his son, Tahath his son," etc.

The extent to which the framer of this list has studied comprehensiveness and conciseness will appear from the fact, which no one would suspect unless informed from other sources, that while the general law which prevails in it is that of descent from father to son, the third, fourth and fifth names represent brothers. This is shown by a comparison with Exodus 6:24 and the parallel genealogy, 1 Chronicles 6:36-37. So that the true line of descent is the following:

Verses 22-24	*Verses 37-38*
Kohath	Kohath
Amminadab	Izhar
Korah	Korah
Assir	
Elkanah	
Ebiasaph	Ebiasaph
Assir	Assir
Tahath, etc.	Tahath, etc.

The circumstance that the son of Kohath is called in one list Amminadab and in the other Izhar is no real discrepancy and can create no embarrassment since it is no unusual thing for the same person to have two names. Witness Abram and Abraham, Jacob and Israel, Joseph and Zaphenath-paneah (Gen. 41:45); Joshea, Jehoshua or Joshua,

(Num. 13:16) and Jeshua (Neh. 8:17); Gideon and Jerubbaal (Judg. 6:32), Solomon and Jedidiah (2 Sam. 12:24), Azariah and Uzziah (2 Kings 15:1, 13); Daniel and Belteshazzar, Hananiah, Mishael, Azariah and Shadrach, Meshach, Abednego (Dan. 1:7); Saul and Paul, Thomas and Didymus, Cephas and Peter, and in profane history Cyaxares and Darius, Octavianus and Augustus, Napoleon and Bonaparte, Feretti and Pius IX.

Genealogy of Moses and Aaron

The genealogy of Moses and Aaron is thus stated in the sixth chapter of Exodus:

> And these are the names of the sons of Levi according to their generations; Gershon, and Kohath, and Merari: and the years of the life of Levi were an hundred and thirty and seven years. The sons of Gershon. . . . And the sons of Kohath; Amram, and Izhar, and Hebron, and Uzziel; and the years of the life of Kohath were an hundred and thirty and three years. And the sons of Merari. . . . And Amram took him Jochebed his father's sister to wife; and she bare him Aaron and Moses: and the years of the life of Amram were an hundred and thirty and seven years. And the sons of Izhar. . . . And the sons of Uzziel. . . . (vv. 16-22)

There is abundant proof that this genealogy has been condensed, as we have already seen that so many others have been, by the dropping of some of the less important names.

This is afforded, in the first place, by parallel genealogies of the same period; as that of Bezaleel (1 Chron. 2:18-20), which records seven generations from Jacob; and that of Joshua (1 Chron. 7:23-27), which records eleven. Now it is scarcely conceivable that there should be eleven links in the line of descent from Jacob to Joshua, and only four from Jacob to Moses.

A still more convincing proof is yielded by Numbers 3: 19, 27-28, from which it appears that the four sons of Kohath severally gave rise to the families of the Amramites, the Izharites, the Hebronites and Uzzielites; and that the number of male members of the families of a month old and upward was 8,600 one year after the Exodus. So that, if no abridgment has taken place in the genealogy, the grandfather of Moses had, in the lifetime of the latter, 8,600 descendants of the male sex alone, 2,750 of them being between the ages of thirty and fifty (Num. 4:36).

Another proof, equally convincing, is to be found in the fact that Levi's son, Kohath, was born before the descent into Egypt (Gen. 46:11); and the abode of the children of Israel in Egypt continued 430 years (Ex. 12:40-41). Now as Moses was eighty years old at the Exodus (Ex. 7:7) he must have been born more than 350 years after Kohath, who consequently could not have been his own grandfather.

This genealogy, whose abbreviated character is so clearly established, is of special importance for the immediate purpose of this paper because it might appear, at first sight, as though such an assumption was precluded in the present instance, and as though the letter of Scripture shuts us up to the inevitable conclusion that there were four links, and no more, from Jacob to Moses. The names which are found without deviation in all the genealogies are Jacob, Levi, Kohath, Amram and Moses (Ex. 6:16-20; Num. 3:17-19; 26:57-59; 1 Chron. 6:1-3, 16-18; 23:6, 12-13). Now unquestionably Levi was Jacob's own son. So likewise Kohath was the son of Levi (Gen. 46:11) and born before the descent into Egypt. Amram also was the immediate descendant of Kohath. It does not seem possible, as Kurtz proposed, to insert the missing links between them. For, in the first place, according to Numbers 26:59, "the name of Amram's wife was Jochebed, the daughter of Levi, whom her mother bare to Levi in Egypt," this Jochebed being (Ex. 6:20) Amram's aunt, or his father's sister. Now it is true that "a daughter of Levi" might have the general sense of a descendant of Levi, as the woman healed by our Lord (Luke

13:16) is called "a daughter of Abraham," and her being born to Levi might simply mean that she sprang from him (cf. Gen. 46:25). But these expressions must here be taken in a strict sense, and Jochebed accordingly must have been Levi's own daughter and the sister of Kohath, who must in consequence have been Amram's own father. This appears from a second consideration, namely, that Amram was (Num. 3:27) the father of one of the subdivisions of the Kohathites, these subdivisions springing from Kohath's own children and comprising together 8,600 male descendants. Moses' father surely could not have been the ancestor of one-fourth of this number in Moses' own days.

To avoid this difficulty Thiele and Keil assume that there were two Amrams, one the son of Kohath, another the father of Moses, who was a more remote descendant but bore the same name with his ancestor. This relieves the embarrassment created by the Amramites (Num. 3:27) but is still liable to that which arises from making Jochebed the mother of Moses. And further, the structure of the genealogy in Exodus 6 is such as to make this hypothesis unnatural and improbable. Verse 16 names the three sons of Levi, Gershom, Kohath and Merari, verses 17-19, the sons of each in their order; verses 20-22, the children of Kohath's sons; verses 23-24, contain descendants of the next generation, and verse 25 the generation next following. Now according to the view of Thiele and Keil, we must either suppose that the Amram, Izhar and Uzziel of verses 20-22 are all different from the Amram, Izhar and Uzziel of verse 18, or else that Amram, though belonging to a later generation than Izhar and Uzziel, is introduced before them, which the regular structure of the genealogy forbids; and besides, the sons of Izhar and the sons of Uzziel, who are here named, were contemporaries of Moses and Aaron the sons of Amram (Num. 16:1; Lev. 10:4).

The subject may be relieved from all perplexity, however, by observing that Amram and Jochebed were not the immediate parents, but the ancestors of Aaron and Moses. How many generations may have intervened we cannot tell. It is indeed said (Ex. 6:20; Num. 26:59), that Jochebed bare them to Amram. But in the language of the genealogies this simply means that they were descended from her and from Amram. Thus in Genesis 46:18, after recording the sons of Zilpah, her grandsons and her great-grandsons, the writer adds, "These are the sons of Zilpah. . . . and these she bare unto Jacob, even sixteen souls." The same thing recurs in the case of Bilhah (v. 25): "She bare these unto Jacob; all the souls were seven" (cf. also vv. 15, 22). No one can pretend here that the author of this register did not use the terms understandingly of descendants beyond the first generation. In like manner, according to Matthew 1:11, Josias begat his grandson Jechonias, and verse 8, Joram begat his great-great-grandson Ozias. And in Genesis 10: 15-18 Canaan, the grandson of Noah, is said to have begotten several whole nations, the Jebusite, the Amorite, the Girgasite, the Hivite, etc. (cf. also Gen. 25:23; Deut. 4:25; 2 Kings 20:18; Is. 2:2). Nothing can be plainer, therefore, than that, in the usage of the Bible, "to bear" and "to beget" are used in a wide sense to indicate descent, without restriction to the immediate offspring.[4]

It is no serious objection to this view of the case that in Leviticus 10:4 Uzziel, Amram's brother, is called "the uncle of Aaron." The Hebrew word which here is translated "uncle," though often specifically applied to a definite degree of relationship, has, both from etymology and usage, a much wider sense. A great-great-granduncle is still an uncle, and would properly be described by the term used here.

It may also be observed that in the actual history of the birth of Moses his parents are not called Amram and Jochebed. Instead, the text simply says (Ex. 2:1), "And there went a man of the house of Levi, and took to wife a daughter of Levi."

Genealogies of Genesis 5 and 11

After these preliminary observations, which were originally drawn up for another purpose, I come to the more immediate design of the present paper by proceeding to inquire whether the genealogies of Genesis 5 and 11 are necessarily to be considered as complete and embracing all the links in the line of descent from Adam to Noah and from Shem to Abraham. The analogy of the Scripture genealogies is decidedly against such a supposition. In numerous other instances there is incontrovertible evidence of more or less abridgment. This may be the case where various circumstances combine to produce a different impression at the outset. Nevertheless, we have seen that this first impression may be dissipated by a more careful examination and a comparison of collateral data. The result of our investigations thus far is sufficient to show that it is precarious to assume that any biblical genealogy is designed to be strictly continuous, unless it can be subjected to some external tests which prove it to be so. And it is to be observed that the Scriptures furnish no collateral information whatever respecting the period covered by the genealogies now in question. The creation, the Flood, the call of Abraham are great facts which stand out distinctly in primeval sacred history. A few incidents respecting our first parents and their sons Cain and Abel are recorded. Then there is an almost total blank until the Flood, with nothing whatever to fill the gap, and nothing to suggest the length of time intervening but what is found in the genealogy stretching between these two points. And the case is substantially the same from the Flood to Abraham. So far as the biblical records go, we are left not only without adequate data but without any data whatever which can be brought into comparison with these genealogies for the sake of testing their continuity and completeness.

If, therefore, any really trustworthy data can be gathered from any source whatever, from any realm of scientific or antiquarian research, which can be brought into comparison with the genealogies for the sake of determining the question whether they have noted every link in the chain of descent or whether, as in other manifest instances, links have been omitted, such data should be welcomed and the comparison fearlessly made. Science would simply perform the office, in this instance, which information gathered from other parts of Scripture is unhesitatingly allowed to do in regard to those genealogies previously examined.

And it may be worth noting here that a single particular in which a comparison may be instituted between the primeval history of man and Genesis 5, suggests especial caution before affirming the absolute completeness of the latter. The letter of the genealogical record (v. 3), if we were dependent on it alone, might naturally lead us to infer that Seth was Adam's first child. But we know from chapter 4 that he had already had two sons, Cain and Abel, and from 4:17 that he must have had a daughter, and from 4:14 that he had probably had several sons and daughters whose families had swollen to a considerable number before Adam's one hundred and thirtieth year in which Seth was born. Yet of all this the genealogy gives us no inkling.

No Summation of These Genealogies in Scripture

Is there not, however, a peculiarity in the construction of these genealogies which forbids our applying to them an inference drawn from others not so constructed? The fact that each member of the series is said to have begotten the one next succeeding, is, in the light of the wide use of this term which we have discovered in other cases, no evidence of itself that links have not been omitted. But do not the chronological statements introduced into these genealogies oblige us to regard them as necessarily continuous? Why should the author be so particular to state, in every case, with unfailing regularity, the age of each patriarch at the birth of his son, unless it was his design thus to construct a chronology of this entire period and to afford his readers the necessary elements for a computation of the interval from the creation to the deluge and from the deluge to Abraham? And if this was his design, he must of course have aimed to make his list complete. The omission of even a single name would create an error.

But are we really justified in supposing that the author of the genealogies entertained such a purpose? It is a noticeable fact that he never puts them to such a use himself. He nowhere sums these numbers, nor suggests their summation. No chronological statement is deduced from these genealogies either by him or by any inspired writer. There is no computation anywhere in Scripture of the time that elapsed from the creation or from the deluge, as there is from the descent into Egypt to the Exodus (Ex. 12:40), or from the Exodus to the building of the temple (1 Kings 6:1). And if the numbers in these genealogies are for the sake of constructing a chronology, why are numbers introduced which have no possible relation to such a purpose? Why are we told how long each patriarch lived after the birth of his son, and what was the entire period of his life? These numbers are given with the same regularity as the age of each at the birth of his son and they are of no use in making up a chronology of the period. They merely afford us a conspectus of individual lives. And for this reason, doubtless, they are recorded. They exhibit in these selected examples the original term of human life. They show what it was in the ages before the Flood. They show how it was afterwards gradually narrowed down. But in order to do this it was not necessary that every individual should be named in the line from Adam to Noah and from Noah to Abraham, nor anything approaching it. A series of specimen lives, with the appropriate numbers attached, was all that was required. And, so far as appears, this is all that has been furnished us. And if this be the case, the notion of basing a chronological computation upon these genealogies is a fundamental mistake. It is putting them to a purpose that they were not designed to subserve and to which from the method of their construction they are not adapted. When it is said, for example, that "Enoch lived ninety years and begat Kenan," the well-established usage of the word "begat" makes this statement equally true and equally accordant with analogy, whether Kenan was himself born when Enoch was ninety years of age, or one was born from whom Kenan sprang. These genealogies may yield us the minimum length of time that it is possible to accept for the period that they cover; but they can make no account of the duration represented by the names that have been dropped from the register as needless for the author's particular purpose.

Analogous to Genealogy of Moses

The abode of the children of Israel in Egypt affords for our present purpose the best Scripture parallel to the periods now under consideration. The greater part of this term of 430 years is left blank in the sacred history. A few incidents are mentioned at the beginning connected with the descent of Jacob and his family into Egypt and their settlement there. And at its close, mention is made of some incidents in the life of Moses and the events leading to the Exodus. But with these exceptions no account is given of this long period. The interval is only bridged by a genealogy extending from Levi to Moses and Aaron and their contemporaries among their immediate relatives (Ex. 6:16-26). This genealogy records the length of each man's life in the principal line of descent: Levi (v. 16), Kohath (v. 18), Amram (v. 20). The correspondence in the points just indicated with the genealogies of Genesis 5 and 11, and the periods which they cover, is certainly remarkable. And as they proceeded from the same pen, we may fairly infer from the similarity of construction a similarity of design. Now it has been shown already that the genealogy from Levi to Moses cannot have recorded all the links in that line of descent, and that it could not, therefore, have been intended to be used as a basis of chronological computation. This is rendered absolutely certain by the explicit statement in Exodus 12:40. It further appears from the fact that the numbers given in this genealogy exhibit the longevity of the patriarchs named, but cannot be so concatenated as to sum up the entire period; thus suggesting the inference that the numbers in the other genealogies, with which we are now concerned, were given with a like design, and not with the view of enabling the reader to construct the chronology.

Archaeology against Completeness of Genealogies

In so far as a valid argument can be drawn from the civilization of Egypt, its monuments and records, to show that the interval between the deluge and the call of Abraham must have been greater than that yielded by the genealogy in Genesis 11, the argument is equally valid against the assumption that this genealogy was intended to supply the elements for a chronological computation. For altogether apart from his inspiration, Moses could not have made a mistake here. He was brought up at the court of Pharaoh and was learned in all the wisdom of the Egyptians, of which his legislation and the marvelous table of the affinities of nations in Genesis 10, at once the admiration and despair of ethnologists, furnish independent proof. He lived in the glorious period of the great Egyptian monarchy. Its monuments were then in their freshness and completeness. None of the irreparable damage, which time and ruthless barbarism have since wrought, had been suffered then. The fragmentary records, which scholars are now laboriously struggling to unravel and combine, with their numerous gaps and hopeless obscurities, were then in their integrity, and well understood. Egypt's claim to a hoary antiquity was far better known to Moses, and he was in a position to gain a far more intelligent comprehension of it than is possible at present; for exuberant materials were ready at his hand, of which only a scanty and disordered remnant now survives. If, then, Egyptian antiquity contradicts the current chronology, it simply shows that this chronology is based upon an unfounded assumption. It rests upon a fundamentally mistaken interpretation of the ante-Abrahamic genealogy and assigns a meaning to it which Moses could never have intended that it should have.

As is well known, the texts of the Septuagint and of the Samaritan Pentateuch vary systematically from the Hebrew in both the genealogies of Genesis 5 and 11. According to the chronologies based on these texts respectively, the interval between the Flood and the birth of Abraham was 292 (Hebrew), 942 (Samaritan) or 1,172 years (Septuagint). Some have been disposed in this state of the case to adopt the chronology drawn from the Septuagint, as affording here the needed relief. But the superior accuracy of the Hebrew text in this instance, as well as generally elsewhere, can be incontrovertibly established. This resource, then, is a broken reed. It might, however, be plausibly imagined, and has in fact been maintained, that these changes were made by the Septuagint translators or others for the sake of accommodating the Mosaic narrative to the imperative demands of the accepted Egyptian antiquity. But if this be so, it is only a further confirmation of the argument already urged, that the ante-Abrahamic genealogy cannot have been intended by Moses as a basis of chronological computation. He knew as much of the age of Egypt as the Septuagint translators or any in their day. And if so brief a term as this genealogy yields was inadmissible in their judgment and they felt constrained to enlarge it by the addition of nearly nine centuries, is it not clear that Moses never could have intended that the genealogy should be so interpreted?

Furthermore, it seems to me worthy of consideration whether the original intent with which these textual changes were made, was after all a chronological one. The principle by which they are obviously and uniformly governed, is rather suggestive of a disposition to make a more symmetrical division of individual lives than to protract the entire period. The effect of these changes upon the chronology may have been altogether unintentional, not deliberate.

Thus in the Hebrew text of Genesis 5, the ages of different patriarchs at the birth of a son named are quite irregular and vary from sixty-five to one hundred and eighty-seven. But the versions seek to bring them into closer conformity and to introduce something like a regular gradation. The Septuagint proceeds on the assumption that patriarchs of such enormous longevity should be nearly two centuries old at the birth of their son. Accordingly, when, in the Hebrew, they fall much below this standard, one hundred years are added to the number preceding the birth of the son and the same amount deducted from the number following his birth; the total length of each life is thus preserved without change, the proportion of its different parts alone being altered. The Samaritan, on the other hand, assumes a gradual diminution in the ages of successive patriarchs prior to the birth of their son, none rising to a century after the first two. When, therefore, the number in the Hebrew text exceeds one hundred, one hundred is deducted and the same amount added to the years after the son was born. In the case of Lamech the reduction is greater still in order to effect the necessary diminution. The table on page 122 shows the years assigned to the several antediluvian patriarchs before the birth of their sons in these several texts.

A simple glance at these numbers is sufficient to show that the Hebrew is the original, from which the others diverge on the one side or the other according to the principle which they have severally adopted. It likewise creates a strong presumption that the object contemplated in these changes was to make the lives more symmetrical, rather than to effect an alteration in the chronology.

	Hebrew	*Septuagint*	*Samaritan*
Adam	130	230	130
Seth	105	205	105
Enosh	90	190	90
Kenan	70	170	70
Mahalaleel	65	165	65
Jared	162	162	62
Enoch	65	165	65
Methuselah	187	167 (187)[5]	67
Lamech	182	188	53
Noah	600	600	600

Symmetry of the Genealogies

The structure of the genealogies in Genesis 5 and 11 also favors the belief that they do not register all the names in these respective lines of descent. Their regularity seems to indicate intentional arrangements. Each genealogy includes ten names, Noah being the tenth from Adam, and Terah the tenth from Noah. And each ends with a father having three sons, as is likewise the case with the Cainite genealogy (4:17-22). The Sethite genealogy (chapter 5) culminates in its seventh member, Enoch who "walked with God, and he was not, for God took him." The Cainite genealogy also culminates in its seventh member, Lamech, with his polygamy, bloody revenge and boastful arrogance. The genealogy descending from Shem divides evenly at its fifth member, Peleg: and "in his days was the earth divided." Now as the adjustment of the genealogy in Matthew 1 into three periods of fourteen generations each is brought about by dropping the requisite number of names, it seems in the highest degree probable that the symmetry of these primitive genealogies is artificial rather than natural. It is much more likely that this definite number of names fitting into a regular scheme has been selected as sufficiently representing the periods to which they belong, than that all these striking numerical coincidences should have happened to occur in these successive instances.

It may further be added that if the genealogy in chapter 11 is complete, Peleg, who marks the entrance of a new period, died while all his ancestors from Noah onward were still living. Indeed Shem, Arphaxad, Selah and Eber must all have outlived not only Peleg, but all the generations following as far as and including Terah. The whole impression of the narrative in Abraham's days is that the Flood was an event long since past and that the actors in it had passed away ages before. And yet if a chronology is to be constructed out of this genealogy Noah was for fifty-eight years the contemporary of Abraham, and Shem actually survived him thirty-five years, provided 11:26 is to be taken in its natural sense, that Abraham was born in Terah's seventieth year. This conclusion is well-nigh incredible. The calculation which leads to such a result, must proceed upon a wrong assumption.

On these various grounds we conclude that the Scriptures furnish no data for a chronological computation prior to the life of Abraham; and that the Mosaic records do not fix and were not intended to fix the precise date either of the Flood or of the creation of the world.

Appendix 3

How Long Is the Sixth Day?

R. John Snow

The debate continues to brew in evangelical circles over the creation account in Genesis 1. Over the years, attempts to correlate alleged facts of science with the divine revelation have taken various forms. Relatively recently, however, the gap theory (held by DeHaan, Pink, Scofield and many other Christians) has been demonstrated to be unreliable in its exegetical basis, and most theologians have come to reject this view. Among those who hold to the inspiration of Scripture, the battle over the interpretation of Genesis 1 has tended to narrow down to the question of whether the days of God's creative activity were literal, twenty-four-hour days or figurative days of greater length. Against those who hold the latter view, the charge has been made that the real motivation for such a view is the preconceived notion that scientific "facts" must be correct and the Bible made to fit, whereas if one considers just the Bible, only the literal-day view is possible.[1]

The thesis of this paper is that, aside from the external evidence of present-day scientific observations for determining age, there is adequate *exegetical* evidence to demonstrate that the days of Genesis 1 can be considered long indefinite periods. It is the feeling of the author that this is an area where the Christian needs to display openness, realizing that the intent of Genesis is theological and religious. To be dogmatic in the area of scientific correlation with the Scriptures can be dangerous, opening the door for repeating the errors of theology in the past.

Lessons from History

It is widely recognized that the word *yom* ("day"), as used in the Old Testament has a variety of meanings: a period of light (Gen. 1:5), twenty-four hours (Gen. 1:14b), or longer periods of time as in Genesis 2:4. Young says, "The length of days is not stated; what is important is that each of the days is a period of time which may legitimately be denominated *yom* ('day')."[2] This fact, then, opens the door for the possibility that the days of Genesis 1 represent any of the meanings listed above. The question is, of course, which one (or ones) are intended? Some feel that as yet we cannot know. Francis Schaeffer notes:

> In the light of the word as used in the Bible and the lack of finality of science concerning the problem of dating, in a sense there is no debate because there are no clearly defined terms upon which to debate.[3]

Schaeffer appears to be waiting upon science to determine which way the pendulum will swing. This approach is considered dangerous by others (for example, John C. Whitcomb, Jr., in *The Origin of the Solar System*) and therefore to be avoided.

Indeed, in some circles it seems to be evidence of spirituality to ignore scientific evidence that appears to contradict the "general impression" interpretation of Genesis 1. However, such people should be careful or they may repeat the errors of history rather than learning from them. Galileo was denounced as a heretic for insisting on the Copernican theory of the solar system. Why? Because the Scriptures taught otherwise, according to the leading theologians of the day. Psalm 19 was quoted,[4] and the account of Joshua's long day,[5] as sure scriptural proof that the earth was the center of the universe. A portion of a letter written by Cardinal Bellarmine reads as follows:

> I may add that the man who wrote "The earth abideth forever; the sun also riseth, and the sun goeth down, and hasteth to his place whence he arose," was Solomon, who not only spoke by divine inspiration but was wise and learned, above all others, in human sciences and in the knowledge of created things. As he had all this wisdom from God himself, it is not likely that he would have made a statement contrary to a truth, either proven or capable of proof. If you tell me that Solomon speaks according to appearances, inasmuch as though the sun seems to revolve, it is really the earth that does so . . . But as to the sun and the earth, a wise man has no need to correct his judgment for his experience tells him plainly that the earth is standing still and that his eyes are not deceived when they report that the sun, moon and stars are in motion.[6]

I wonder if many evangelical scholars of today would not have agreed with the Cardinal had they lived in that day, only to suffer the embarrassment of having to revise their hermeneutic later in the light of scientific fact. Galileo in his letter to Castelli (December 13, 1613) very succinctly says:

> Scripture deals with natural matters in such a cursory and allusive way that it looks as though it wanted to remind us that its business is not about them but about the soul and that, as concerns nature, it is willing to adjust its language to the simple minds of the people.[7]

Similar problems in the Bible/science debate arose when Columbus presented his views regarding a spherical earth:

> Columbus was assailed with citations from the Bible and New Testament: The Book of Genesis, the Psalms of David, the Prophets, the Epistles and the Gospels. To these were added the expositions of various saints and commentators: St. Chrysostom, St. Augustine, St. Jerome, St. Gregory, St. Basil, St. Ambrose and Lactantius, a redoubtable champion of the faith.[8]

Why do I mention these historical notes? To point out the real blunders theologians can make (1) by not considering various possibilities of interpretation, and (2) when facts of nature become reasonably certain, not being willing to adopt that interpretation which fits all the truth.

The Events of Day Six

Much of what has been written in favor of literal creative days is limited to Genesis 1 and its use of the numerical adjective, the phrase "evening and morning," and other similar considerations.[9] However, there has been little consideration given to the "close-up view" of creation presented in chapter two of Genesis, which particularly describes the events of day six.

Several events are recorded in Genesis 2 as occurring on day six. The following is a list of these events with appropriate comments in regard to time indications:

(1) "God *formed* man of the dust of the ground, breathed into his nostrils the breath of life, and he became a living soul" (v. 7). An instantaneous act does not seem to be implied here, but rather an action which consumes some time. The first verb used, *yatsar*, means to "mold" or "form." "It is the word that specifically describes the activity of the potter (Jer. 18:2ff)."[10]

(2) God *planted* a garden (v. 8). The notion of planting also suggests activity which involves time. The details are not described, but if an instantaneous act was intended, Moses certainly had vocabulary available (for example, *bara'*, "create") to so indicate. Wild vegetation today is often

planted by birds, wind and other natural phenomena. I suggest that God in his providence worked through such means to produce the beautiful garden as a special place for the man whom he had formed. Verse 9a further expands the notion of time as it says, "God *made to grow* every tree that is pleasant to the sight." The process of growth too was involved in producing this garden in which man would dwell.

(3) God *placed* man in the garden. Perhaps some time was involved here, also, but it would be difficult to suggest a time span or even the process of transportation. Certainly I would agree it is possible that "At the word of the Lord he may have been removed thither."[11]

(4) God said, "I *will make* him a help fit for him" (v. 18b). The future is used, denoting time subsequent to God's pronouncement. This span of time seems to cover the next three events.

(5) All the cattle, birds of the sky and every beast of the field were brought to Adam for naming (vv. 19-20). Certainly some time is involved in this activity. If every one of the approximately 15,000 living species of such animals[12] (not to mention those now extinct) were brought to Adam to be named, it would have taken ten hours if he spent only two seconds on each. Of course, it may be debated whether all present species existed at that time, a point not to be dealt with here, but we must also realize that this "naming" event could not have been a quick, cursory activity and still fit either God's intended result for this event or the proper significance of "naming."

> Ancient thought attached much greater importance to the names than we do. Words were more than a means of communication and the use of appropriate names was anything but arbitrary. Naming an animal properly indicated that one had understood and characterized its properties, that one had established a relationship with it and one's rule over it.[13]

To limit Adam to such a short time as the literal-day interpretation requires is not at all in keeping with this concept of naming.

(6) God caused Adam to go into a deep sleep, and he slept (v. 21). An interval is indicated during which Adam slept so that God could perform an operation. No doubt, the deep sleep was induced so that Adam would not suffer pain, and then so the healing process could take place as directed by God.

(7) God *built* a woman (v. 22b). The word "build" "applies to the fashioning of a structure of some importance; it involves constructive effort."[14] The time indication is evident even though God uses supernatural processes to complete this remarkable act.

It is only natural to ask, How much time transpired as these events took place? Can twenty-four hours be enough? This author feels that it is difficult to conceive of these events occurring in such a short interval without resorting not only to supernatural acts but also to additional explanations such as Adam's superior intelligence to enable him to name the animals so quickly. But the Scriptures nowhere suggest that such additional assumptions are to be made.

It is apparent from the text that Adam and Eve were last in the creative acts of day six and that all the time-consuming events just mentioned are related to Adam. So if the literal-day view is held, Adam does not even have twenty-four hours to become an accomplished zoologist and to recognize that he is missing something—a wife!

The Term Happa'am

Another time-indicator in Genesis 2, suggesting that day six is longer than twenty-four hours and warranting more detailed consideration, is *happa'am* (root *pa'am*) which appears in verse 23. The root form has many meanings ("best," "foot," "anvil," "occurrence") and is used 118 times in the Old Testament. However, when it is used with the article it takes on a time connotation and is translated by

Brown, Driver and Briggs as "now at length."[15]

The translation of Genesis 2:23a is given below for three selected versions, with *happa'am* emphasized:

> And the man said, this is *now* bone of my bones. . . . (NASB)
>
> Then the man said, This *at last* is bone of my bones. . . . (RSV)
>
> And the man said: This now *at length* is bone of my bones. . . . (Leupold)[16]

Leupold, commenting on his translation above, says, "That a being of this sort had been looked for with anticipation appears from the word *happa'am* 'now at length.' "[17] Another commentator says,

> Adam recognized in her the desired companion, welcomed her joyfully as his bride and expressed his joy in a poetic exclamation. The words "this is now" reflect his pleasant surprise as he saw in the woman the fulfillment of his heart's desire.[18]

Lange says, "In contrast with the long missing of his help, he finds *at last* his desire realized."[19]

The question that naturally comes to mind is, How could Adam generate this great desire in such a short time, if the literal-day view is correct? To develop such a longing, that is, to know that one is missing something such as human companionship, does not generally become a psychological reality until a time has passed substantially greater than allowable with a literal-day interpretation. God induced this desire by having Adam observe the animals, and in the process of time this desire and knowledge of his lack came (v. 20). "The words 'This is now bone . . .' are expressive of joyous astonishment at the suitable helpmeet. . . ."[20] This exclamation springs from a desire for human companionship greater than could develop in only a few hours. It is to be noted that "the creation of animals does not alleviate man's need for a *real* partner. They do not overcome man's basic loneliness. For that reason God creates the woman."[21]

Now the above interpretation is not only supported by the consideration of the time necessary to develop such desire or emotion, but it is also substantiated by the very usage of the word *happa'am* elsewhere. The evaluation of the references which follow will bear this out:

Genesis 29:34-35: The context of this passage deals with Leah, who had been given over to Jacob as his wife by the crafty devices of Laban (vv. 24-25). Jacob loved not Leah, but rather Rachel. Leah, being unloved, became despondent and sought Jacob's love through child-bearing. After having borne a third son to him, she says, "Now (*happa'am*) this time will my husband become attached to me . . ." (29:34b). That is to say, after such a long time and three children, my husband will surely find favor with me. The emotional time-content is quite evident in this passage.

Genesis 30:20: The context here is again that of Leah and her relationship to Jacob. Having three sons did not change his relationship to her, so she continues to bear children by him. After son number six, she still greatly desires to win his favor and exclaims: "Now (*happa'am*) will my husband dwell with me" (30:20b). Again the word *happa'am* denotes a substantial time-period.

Genesis 46:30: This verse falls within the life of Joseph, when Jacob is finally reunited with his favorite son. His great remorse over Joseph's alleged death remains with him from the time his sons relate the sad story (Gen. 37:34). The many years that elapse between the events of chapters 37 and 46 give rise to the expression of 46:30b: "Now (*happa'am*) let me die, since I have seen thy face. . . ."

Judges 15:3: Samson had been deceived by his Philistine bride to tell her the riddle of the honey and the lion, causing him to lose both a wager and a triumph over the Philistine oppressors. Samson angrily departs before the marriage is consummated, only to return later and find that his wife had been given to another. As a result he becomes really angry, and exclaims, "Now (*happa'am*) shall I be more blameless . . ." (15:3). The passage suggests that Samson has been seeking revenge for some time, and now at last he feels justified in doing so (which he immediately does).

Judges 16:18: Delilah has schemed long and hard to learn the source of Samson's strength. Finally Samson succumbs to the pressure and gives in to her. Then she says to the soldiers outside, "Come up this once (*happa'am*) for he hath shown me" (16:18b). Emotion is expressed as the result of a time-consuming series of events.

Exodus 9:27: After a long series of plagues Pharaoh appears to be softening with regard to the release of the Israelites. He finally exclaims, "I have sinned this time (*happa'am*) . . ." (9:27b), or as Brown, Driver and Briggs render it, "Now at length I have sinned."[22] Here the word takes on a definite time reference, spanning the period of the plagues.

The word *happa'am* is also used in Genesis 18:32, Exodus 10:17, Judges 6:39 and 16:28. In these passages it occurs with the adverb *'ak* and is translated "only this once."[23] In each case it is used to terminate a time period of some length. Only in one case, Genesis 18:32, where Abraham intercedes for Sodom that God would withhold his judgment, is this period shorter than a few weeks, and here the strong emotional climax may build quickly because Abraham is bargaining with God.

From all these uses of *happa'am*, we see that it functions as a terminating expression for an emotional build-up which has been developing within a person over an extended time. In all six cases without the adverb, and in all but one with it, this time involves weeks and sometimes years, during which the desire or emotion rises to a climax.

John Calvin notes:

> In using the expression *happa'am*, Adam indicates that something had been wanting to him; as if he had said, "Now at length I have obtained a suitable companion, who is part of the substance of my flesh, and in whom I

behold, as it were, another self."[24]

Even though the length of time that passed from God's bringing the animals before Adam to be named until Adam awoke from his deep sleep is not specified, it seems unreasonable, impractical and exegetically unwarranted to insist that this interval be limited to only a few hours. Gleason Archer expresses the time factors of day six by noting:

1. Adam was given the responsibility of tending the Garden of Eden for some length of time until God observed him to be lonely.
2. God then granted him the fellowship of all the beasts and animals of the earth, giving them all names.
3. Loneliness is still apparent—so God fashions a wife—by a rib taken from deep sleep.[25]

Archer then goes on to ask if all the above events occurred in twenty-four hours, concluding: "Obviously the 'days' of chapter 1 are intended to represent stages of unspecified length, not literal twenty-four-hour days."[26]

Conclusion

God's activity in bringing the earth into existence with all its intricate detail and physical properties is so astounding that God has told us ultimately it is "through faith we understand that the worlds were framed by the word of God, so that the things which are seen were not made of the things which do appear" (Heb. 11:3). Hence as science seeks to discover the secrets of the formation of the eons[27] (which seems to be a legitimate enterprise in view of Gen. 1:28 and Ps. 19:1), there is still the necessity of faith. This cannot be avoided. Faith must be the ultimate touchstone of Christian inquiry into the matter of creation and origins. Yet as the facts of language and nature are discovered, it is important to remember a principle given by Charles Hodge: "If the ordinary sense brings the Mosaic account into conflict with facts, and another sense would avoid such conflict, then it is obligatory on us to adopt the other."[28]

It is the "ordinary sense" of Genesis 1 that is usually argued in favor of a twenty-four-hour-day view of creation week. It has been shown in this paper that "another sense" is a legitimate understanding for day six. May it not also be the proper understanding of the other days also?

In light of the fact that there are evidences in support of both sides of the "day" question, may the saints be diligent in searching the Scriptures and in recognizing those areas which are unknown. And may they be willing to submit to the teaching of God as he chooses to reveal these things, whether through a Galileo or a theologian, testing each teaching whether it be of God.

Notes

Introduction

[1]R. Hooykaas, *Religion and the Rise of Modern Science* (Grand Rapids: William B. Eerdmans Publishing Co., 1972).

[2]Herbert Butterfield, *The Origins of Modern Science: 1300-1800*, revised ed. (New York: Free Press, 1965), pp. 177-78.

[3]E.g., F. Donald Eckelmann, "Geology," in *The Encounter between Christianity and Science*, ed. Richard H. Bube (Grand Rapids: William B. Eerdmans Publishing Co., 1968), pp. 168-69.

[4]E.g., Alfred M. Rehwinkel, *The Flood*, Revised ed. (St. Louis: Concordia Publishing House, 1957), p. 24.

[5]This term was apparently coined by Bernard Ramm. See his *The Christian View of Science and Scripture* (Grand Rapids: William B. Eerdmans Publishing Co., 1954), pp. 112ff.

[6]Edwin R. Thiele, *The Mysterious Numbers of the Hebrew Kings*, 2nd ed. (Grand Rapids: William B. Eerdmans Publishing Co., 1965).

Chapter 1

[1]See George Abell, *Exploration of the Universe*, 3rd ed. (New York: Holt, Rinehart and Winston, 1975), chaps. 19, 20, 21, 23, 25, 26, 33; Franklyn W. Cole, *Fundamental Astronomy* (New York: John Wiley and Sons, 1974), chaps. 11, 12, 14; or Lloyd Motz and Anneta Duveen, *Essentials of Astronomy* (Belmont, CA: Wadsworth Publishing Co., 1966), chaps. 15, 30; on a somewhat more advanced level, Martin Harwit, *Astrophysical Concepts* (New York: John Wiley and Sons, 1973), chap. 2.

[2]William D. Metz, "Research News," *Science*, 181 (21 Sept 73), 1156.

[3]John C. Whitcomb, Jr. and Henry M. Morris, *The Genesis Flood* (Philadelphia: Presbyterian and Reformed Publishing Co., 1961), p. 369.

[4]*Science and Scripture*, (Mar-Apr 71), 22; Whitcomb and Morris, *Genesis Flood*, pp. 369-70.

[5]P. Moon and D. E. Spencer, "Binary Stars and the Velocity of Light," *Journal of the Optical Society of America*, 43 (Aug 53), 635-41.

[6]Bart J. Bok and Priscilla Bok, *The Milky Way*, 4th ed. (Cambridge: Harvard University Press, 1974), p. 250.

[7]R. C. Newman, "Hierarchical Cosmologies: A New Trend?" *Journal of the American Scientific Affiliation,* 24, (Mar 72), 4-8.

[8]William D. Metz, "Speaking of Science," *Science*, 178 (10 Nov 72), 601.

[9]See Robert Newman's discussion in "Hierarchical Cosmologies: A New Trend?"

[10]Robert Jastrow and Malcolm Thompson, *Astronomy: Fundamentals and Frontiers*, 2nd ed. (New York: John Wiley and Sons, 1974), pp. 270-71; Abell, *Exploration of the Universe*, pp. 663-65.

[11]See Harwit, *Astrophysical Concepts*, chap. 8.

[12]The life cycle of stars is discussed in most recent astronomy texts, e.g., Abell, *Exploration of the Universe*, chaps. 30, 31; Cole, *Fundamental Astronomy*, chap. 12; Harwit, *Astrophysical Concepts,* chap. 8; Motz and Duveen, *Essentials of Astronomy*, chap. 23.

[13]Abell, *Exploration of the Universe*, p. 563; Motz and Duveen, *Essentials of Astronomy*, p. 504.

[14]Jastrow and Thompson, *Astronomy*, pp. 163-69, 263; Abell, *Exploration of the Universe,* pp. 556, 563-67.
[15]Abell, *Exploration of the Universe,* p. 595; Cole, *Fundamental Astronomy,* p. 262.
[16]Jastrow and Thompson, *Astronomy*, pp. 161, 189, 194.
[17]E. L. Schatzman, *The Structure of the Universe* (New York: McGraw-Hill Book Co., 1968), p. 116; Abell, *Exploration of the Universe*, p. 560.
[18]John A. Wood, *Meteorites and the Origin of Planets* in *Earth and Planetary Science Series*, ed. Patrick M. Hurley (New York: McGraw-Hill Book Co., 1968), chap. 4.
[19]Cole, *Fundamental Astronomy*, pp. 147-48.
[20]Henry Faul, *Ages of Rocks, Planets, and Stars* in *Earth and Planetary Science Series*, ed. Patrick M. Hurley (New York: McGraw-Hill Book Co., 1966), p. 11.
[21]Harwit, *Astrophysical Concepts*, p. 477.
[22]Faul, pp. 4, 11. Electron capture is the opposite of beta decay; here the nucleus captures an inner electron "orbiting" the atom. The two decay schemes of uranium listed involve a series of alpha and beta decays.
[23]Ibid., pp. 11-13; J. O. D. Johnston, "The Problems of Radiocarbon Dating," *Palestine Exploration Quarterly,* 105 (1973), 13-26.
[24]Faul, chap. 6; Don L. Eicher, *Geologic Time* in *Foundations of Earth Science Series*, ed. A. Lee McAlester (Englewood Cliffs, N. J.: Prentice-Hall, Inc., 1968), pp. 137-38.
[25]Faul, chap. 4.
[26]Ibid., chap. 3; Eicher, pp. 126-27.
[27]R. D. Evans, *The Atomic Nucleus* (New York: McGraw-Hill Book Co., 1955), p. 390.
[28]Faul, pp. 23-28.
[29]Racemization refers to the fact that predominantly "left-handed" molecules decay toward a state in which there are an equal number of "left-handed" and "right-handed" molecules.

Chapter 2

[1]William K. Hartmann, *Moons and Planets: An Introduction to Planetary Science* (Belmont, CA: Wadsworth Publishing Co., 1972), pp. 64-65.
[2]Ibid., table 10-1, p. 224.
[3]Motz and Duveen, *Essentials of Astronomy*, p. 230.
[4]H. P. Berlage, *The Origin of the Solar System* (Oxford: Pergamon Press, Ltd., 1968), pp. 48-51.
[5]Pluto is an exception, perhaps an escaped satellite of Neptune.
[6]Hartmann, *Moons and Planets*, pp. 235-37.
[7]Ibid., p. 264.
[8]R. F. Flint and B. J. Skinner, *Physical Geology* (New York: John Wiley and Sons, 1974), chap. 18.
[9]Hartmann, *Moons and Planets*, chaps. 10-12.

Chapter 3

[1]See, for example, Elske Smith and Kenneth Jacobs, *Introductory Astronomy and Astrophysics* (Philadelphia: W. B. Saunders Co., 1973), pp. 108-09; Hartmann, *Moons and Planets*, chap. 4; Berlage, *Origin of the Solar System*, p. 10 passim.
[2]Donald W. Patten, *The Biblical Flood and the Ice Epoch* (Seattle: Pacific Meridan Publishing Co., 1966).

[3]Immanuel Velikovsky, *Worlds in Collision* (New York: Doubleday, 1950).
[4]R. C. Newman, "The Astrophysics of *Worlds in Collision*," *Journal of the American Scientific Affiliation*, 25 (Dec. 1973), 147-48.
[5]Ibid., p. 148.
[6]R. A. Lyttleton, "On the Formation of Planets from a Solar Nebula," *Monthly Notices of the Royal Astronomical Society*, 158 (1972), 463-83.
[7]Smith and Jacobs, *Introductory Astronomy and Astrophysics*, p. 108.
[8]Motz and Duveen, *Essentials of Astronomy*, p. 623.
[9]Hartmann, *Moons and Planets*, pp. 98-101, 371-73.
[10]Smith and Jacobs, *Introductory Astronomy and Astrophysics*, pp. 108-09.
[11]Fred Hoyle, *Frontiers of Astronomy* (New York: Mentor, 1957), chap. 6.
[12]See Bart J. Bok, "The Birth of Stars" in *New Frontiers in Astronomy*, ed. Owen Gingerich (San Francisco: W. H. Freeman and Co., 1975), pp. 127-40.
[13]Wood, *Meteorites and the Origin of Planets*, pp. 88-90.
[14]Newman, "Hierarchical Cosmologies," pp. 6-7.
[15]Abell, *Exploration of the Universe*, p. 558; Cole, *Fundamental Astronomy*, p. 322; Jastrow and Thompson, *Astronomy*, pp. 171-72.
[16]Abell, *Exploration of the Universe*, pp. 586-87; Motz and Duveen, *Essentials of Astronomy*, p. 406.
[17]Abell, *Exploration of the Universe*, pp. 556-57; a more technical discussion in Harwit, *Astrophysical Concepts*, pp. 95-97.
[18]E.g., see Konrad B. Krauskopf and Arthur Beiser, *Fundamentals of Physical Science*, 6th ed. (New York: McGraw-Hill Book Co., 1971), pp. 129-30.
[19]T. G. Cowling, *Magnetohydrodynamics* (New York: Interscience, 1957), pp. 6-8.
[20]Lyttleton, "Formation of Planets," pp. 463, 473, 482.
[21]Wood, *Meteorites and the Origin of Planets*, p. 109; Jastrow and Thompson, *Astronomy*, pp. 340-41.
[22]Berlage, *Origin of the Solar System*, sections 56-74, has a number of interesting suggestions in this area; see also Hartmann, *Moons and Planets*, pp. 119-20.
[23]Jastrow and Thompson, *Astronomy*, pp. 365-66; Hartmann, *Moons and Planets*, pp. 256-62.
[24]Jastrow and Thompson, *Astronomy*, pp. 366-67; Hartmann, *Moons and Planets*, pp. 217-21.
[25]Hartmann, *Moons and Planets*, p. 336.
[26]Von R. Eshleman, "The Atmospheres of Mars and Venus," in *Frontiers of Astronomy*, ed. Owen Gingerich (San Francisco: W. H. Freeman and Co., 1970), pp. 48-58.
[27]Ibid., pp. 48, 58; Hartmann, *Moons and Planets*, p. 336.
[28]Continental drift is discussed in any recent geology text, e.g., Flint and Skinner, *Physical Geology*, chap. 18. For more detailed discussions, see P. J. Wyllie, *The Dynamic Earth* (New York: John Wiley and Sons, 1971) or A. Hallam, *A Revolution in the Earth Sciences* (Oxford: Clarendon Press, 1973).
[29]Hartmann, *Moons and Planets*, pp. 275, 279; Flint and Skinner, *Physical Geology*, pp. 360-66.

Chapter 4

[1]The apocryphal book of Jubilees purports to give a complete chronology from creation in terms of the fifty-year jubilee cycles. See R. H. Charles, *Apocrypha and Pseudepigrapha of the Old Testament* (Oxford: Clarendon Press, 1913), II, 1-82.
[2]E.g., see Hippolytus, *On Daniel*, 2.4.

[3]James Ussher, *Annales Veteris et Novi Testamenti* (1650-54).
[4]Cited in A. D. White, *A History of the Warfare of Science with Theology in Christendom* (New York: Macmillan, 1896; reprint ed., New York: Dover, 1960), I, 9.
[5]William Henry Green, "Primeval Chronology," *Bibliotheca Sacra* 47 (1890), 285-303; recently reprinted in Walter C. Kaiser, ed., *Classical Evangelical Essays in Old Testament Interpretation* (Grand Rapids: Baker Book House, 1972).
[6]E.g., Henry M. Morris, *Biblical Cosmology and Modern Science* (Grand Rapids: Baker Book House, 1970), pp. 66-71, 79-81; John C. Whitcomb, Jr., *The Early Earth* (Grand Rapids: Baker Book House, 1972), pp. 107-11.

Chapter 5

[1]J. Oliver Buswell, Jr., *A Systematic Theology of the Christian Religion* (Grand Rapids: Zondervan Publishing House, 1962), I, 135-37.
[2]Newman, "Hierarchical Cosmologies," pp. 4-8.
[3]See Edward J. Young, *Studies in Genesis One* (Philadelphia: Presbyterian and Reformed Publishing Co., 1964) for a more detailed discussion of this interpretation.
[4]Robert C. Newman, "The Biblical Teaching on the Firmament" (S.T.M. thesis, Biblical Theological Seminary, 1972).
[5]Francis Brown, S. R. Driver and Charles A. Briggs, *A Hebrew and English Lexicon of the Old Testament* (Oxford: Clarendon Press, 1907), pp. 75-76.
[6]*Zondervan Pictoral Bible Encyclopedia*, s.v. "Hebrew Language," by G. L. Archer; *International Standard Bible Encyclopedia*, s.v. "Language of the Old Testament," by T. H. Weir.
[7]Brown, Driver and Briggs, *Lexicon*, p. 1062.
[8]William L. Holladay, *A Concise Hebrew and Aramaic Lexicon of the Old Testament* (Grand Rapids: Eerdmans, 1971), p. 386.
[9]Brown, Driver and Briggs, *Lexicon*, p. 96.
[10]Holladay, *Lexicon*, p. 34.
[11]Alfred Rahlfs, ed., *Septuaginta*, 7th ed. (Stuttgart: Württenbergische Bibelanstalt, 1962), ad loc.
[12]Bart J. Bok, "The Birth of Stars" in *New Frontiers in Astronomy*, ed. Owen Gingerich (San Francisco: W. H. Freeman and Co., 1975), p. 130.
[13]For a detailed treatment, see Newman, *The Biblical Firmament.*
[14]*Evolution and the Origin of Life* (Del Mar, CA: CRM Educational Films, 1973).

Appendix I

[1]Reprinted, with author's corrections, from the *Journal of the American Scientific Affiliation*, vol. 27, no. 4, 145-152 (1975) by permission. Copyright 1975 by American Scientific Affiliation. The author of this appendix has recently completed a 270-page book, *God's Time-Records in Ancient Sediments,* containing numerous examples, with illustrations and further explanations, of most of the sections appearing in this appendix. This book may be ordered from Crystal Press, 1909 Proctor St., Flint, MI 48504.

Appendix II

[1]Reprinted, with headings added, from *Bibliotheca Sacra*, 47 (1890), 285-303. Scripture references are KJV. [2]W. H. Green, *The Pentateuch Vindicated from the Aspersions of Bishop Colenso* (1863), p. 128n. [3]He is called in 1 Chronicles 24:20 a son of Amram, the ancestor of Moses; for Shubael and Shebuel are in all probability mere orthographic variations of the same name. [4]In Ruth 4:17 Ruth's child is called "a son born to Naomi," who was Ruth's mother-in-law and

not even an ancestor of the child in the strict sense. Zerubbabel is called familiarly the son of Shealtiel (Ezr. 3:2; Hag. 1:1), and is so stated to be in the genealogies of both Matthew 1:12 and Luke 3:27, though in reality he was his nephew (1 Chron. 3:17-19). That descent as reckoned in genealogies is not always that of actual parentage appears from the comparison of the ancestry of our Lord as given by Matthew and by Luke. [5]The number varies in different manuscripts.

Appendix III

[1]Alva J. McClain, *Christian Theology: God and the World*, with revisions by John C. Whitcomb, Jr. and Charles R. Smith (Winona Lake, IN: Grace Theological Seminary, n.d.), p. 29. [2]Edward J. Young, "The Days of Genesis," *The Westminster Theological Journal* 25 (1963), 170. [3]Francis A. Schaeffer, *Genesis in Space and Time* (Downers Grove, IL: InterVarsity Press, 1972), p. 57. [4]Georgio DeSantillana, *The Crime of Galileo* (Chicago: University of Chicago Press, 1955), p. 54. [5]James Broderick, *Galileo: The Man, His Works, His Misfortunes* (New York: Harper & Row, 1964), p. 87. [6]DeSantillana, *Crime of Galileo*, p. 100. [7]Ibid., p. 41. [8]Charles Duff, *The Truth about Columbus and the Discovery of America* (London: Jarrolds Publishers, 1936), p. 49. [9]McClain, *Christian Theology*, p. 20. [10]H. C. Leupold, *Exposition of Genesis* (Grand Rapids: Baker Book House, 1942) 1:115. [11]Ibid., p. 118. [12]Lord Rothschild, *A Classification of Living Animals* (New York: John Wiley and Sons, 1961), pp. 4-5. [13]Aldert Van Der Ziel, *Genesis and Scientific Inquiry* (Minneapolis: T. S. Denison and Co., Inc., 1965), p. 59. [14]Leupold, *Exposition of Genesis*, 1:135. [15]Francis Brown, S. R. Driver and Charles A. Briggs, *A Hebrew and English Lexicon of the Old Testament* (Oxford: Clarendon Press, 1907), p. 822. [16]Leupold, *Exposition of Genesis*, 1:135. [17]Ibid., p. 136. [18]Francis D. Nichol, ed., *The Seventh-Day Adventist Bible Commentary* (Washington, DC: Review and Herald Publishing Assoc., 1953), I, 227. [19]John P. Lange, *Commentary on the Holy Scriptures: Genesis* (Grand Rapids: Zondervan Publishing House, 1971), p. 209. [20]C. F. Keil and F. Delitzsch, *Biblical Commentary on the Old Testament* (Grand Rapids: William B. Eerdmans Publishing Co., 1951), I, 90. [21]Van Der Ziel, *Genesis and Scientific Inquiry*, p. 59. [22]Brown, Driver and Briggs, *Lexicon*, p. 822. [23]Ibid. [24]John Calvin, *Commentaries on the Book of Genesis* (Grand Rapids: William B. Eerdmans Publishing Co., 1948), I, 135. [25]Gleason L. Archer, *A Survey of Old Testament Introduction* (Chicago: Moody Press, 1964), p. 176. [26]Ibid. [27]R. C. H. Lenski, *The Interpretation of the Epistle to the Hebrews and the Epistle of James* (Minneapolis: Augsburg Publishing House, 1966), p. 380. [28]Charles Hodge, *Systematic Theology*, (New York: Charles Scribner and Co., 1872), I, 571.

Bibliographies

Articles

Archer, Gleason L. 1975. Hebrew Language. In *Zondervan Pictorial Bible Encyclopedia*, ed. M. C. Tenney, III, 66-76. Grand Rapids: Zondervan.

Bok, Bart J. 1975. The Birth of the Stars. In *New Frontiers in Astronomy*, ed. O. Gingerich, pp. 127-40. San Francisco: W. H. Freeman and Co.

Eckelmann, F. Donald. 1968. Geology. In *The Encounter between Christianity and Science*, ed. R. H. Bube, pp. 135-70. Grand Rapids: Eerdmans.

Eshleman, Von R. 1970. The Atmospheres of Mars and Venus. In *Frontiers of Astronomy*, ed. O. Gingerich, pp. 48-58. San Francisco: W. H. Freeman and Co.

Green, W. H. 1890. Primeval Chronology. *Bibliotheca Sacra* 47: 285-303; recently reprinted in *Classical Evangelical Essays in Old Testament Interpretation,* ed. W. C. Kaiser, Jr., pp. 13-28. Grand Rapids: Baker, 1972.

Johnston, J. O. D. 1973. The Problems of Radiocarbon Dating. *Palestine Exploration Quarterly* 105: 13-26.

Lyttleton, R. A. 1972. On the Formation of Planets from a Solar Nebula. *Monthly Notices of the Royal Astronomical Society* 158: 463-83.

Moon, P. and Spencer, D. E. 1953. Binary Stars and the Velocity of Light. *Journal of the Optical Society of America* 43: 635-41.

Newman, Robert C. 1972. Hierarchical Cosmologies: A New Trend? *Journal of the American Scientific Affiliation* 24: 4-8.

______________. 1973. The Astrophysics of *Worlds in Collision. Journal of the American Scientific Affiliation* 25: 146-51.

Slusher, H. S. 1971. News article in *Science and Scripture* (March-April), p. 22.

Weir, T. H. 1939. Languages of the Old Testament. In *International Standard Bible Encyclopedia*, ed. J. Orr and M. G. Kyle, III, 1832-36. Grand Rapids: Eerdmans.

Books

Astronomy and Physics

Abell, George. 1964. *Exploration of the Universe.* New York: Holt, Rinehart and Winston.

Baker, R. H. and Frederick, L. W. 1971. *Astronomy.* 9th ed. New York: Van Nostrand Reinhold Co.

Berlage, H. P. 1968. *The Origin of the Solar System.* Oxford: Pergamon Press.

Bok, B. J. and Bok, P. 1974. *The Milky Way.* 4th ed. Cambridge, MA: Harvard University Press.

Cole, F. W. 1974. *Fundamental Astronomy.* New York: Wiley.

Cowling, T. G. 1957. *Magnetohydrodynamics.* New York: Interscience Publishers.

Evans, R. D. 1955. *The Atomic Nucleus.* New York: McGraw-Hill.

Gingerich, O., ed. 1970. *Frontiers of Astronomy.* San Francisco: W. H. Freeman and Co.

_______________, ed. 1975. *New Frontiers of Astronomy.* San Francisco: W. H. Freeman and Co.

Hartmann, W. K. 1972. *Moons and Planets: An Introduction to Planetary Science.* Belmont, CA: Wadsworth.

Harwit, M. 1973. *Astrophysical Concepts.* New York: Wiley.

Hoyle, F. 1957. *Frontiers of Astronomy.* New York: Mentor Books.

_______________. 1962. *Astronomy: A History of Man's Investigations of the Universe.* Garden City, NY: Doubleday.

Jastrow, R., and Thompson, M. H. 1972. *Astronomy: Fundamentals and Frontiers.* New York: Wiley.

Krauskopf, K. B., and Beiser, A. 1971. *Fundamentals of Physical Science.* 6th ed. New York: McGraw-Hill.

Motz, L., and Duveen, A. 1966. *Essentials of Astronomy.* Belmont, CA: Wadsworth.

Schatzman, E. L. 1968. *The Structure of the Universe.* New York: McGraw-Hill Book Co.

Smith, E. V. P., and Jacobs, K. 1973. *Introductory Astronomy and Astrophysics.* Philadelphia: W. B. Saunders Co.

Wood, J. A. 1968. *Meteorites and the Origin of Planets* in *Earth and Planetary Science Series,* ed. P. M. Hurley. New York: McGraw-Hill.

Geology and Earth Sciences

Eicher, D. L. 1968. *Geologic Time* in *Foundations of Earth Science Series,* ed. A. L. McAlester. Englewood Cliffs, NJ: Prentice-Hall.

Faul, H. 1966. *Ages of Rocks, Planets and Stars* in *Earth and Planetary Science Series,* ed. P. M. Hurley. New York: McGraw-Hill.

Flint, R. F., and Skinner, B. J. 1974. *Physical Geology.* New York: Wiley.

Hallam, A. 1973. *A Revolution in the Earth Sciences.* Oxford: Clarendon Press.

Wyllie, P. J. 1971. *The Dynamic Earth.* New York: Wiley.

History of Science

Butterfield, H. 1965. *The Origins of Modern Science: 1300-1800.* New York: Free Press.

Hooykas, R. 1972. *Religion and the Rise of Modern Science.* Grand Rapids: Eerdmans.

Bible and Science

Morris, H. M. 1970. *Biblical Cosmology and Modern Science.* Grand Rapids: Baker.

Newman, R. C. 1972. "The Biblical Teaching on the Firmament." S.T.M. thesis, Biblical Theological Seminary.

Patten, D. W. 1966. *The Biblical Flood and the Ice Epoch.* Seattle: Pacific Meridan.

Ramm, B. 1954. *The Christian View of Science and Scripture.* Grand Rapids: Eerdmans.

Rehwinkel, A. M. 1957. *The Flood.* Rev. ed. St. Louis: Concordia.

Velikovsky, I. 1950. *Worlds in Collision.* New York: Doubleday.

Whitcomb, J. C., Jr. 1972. *The Early Earth.* Grand Rapids: Baker.

Whitcomb, J. C., Jr., and Morris, H. M. 1961. *The Genesis Flood.* Philadelphia: Presbyterian and Reformed.

White, A. D. 1960. *A History of the Warfare of Science with Theology and Christendom.* 2 vols. New York: Dover.

Young, E. J. 1964. *Studies in Genesis One.* Philadelphia: Presbyterian and Reformed.

Other Biblical Areas

Brown, F., Driver, S. R., and Briggs, C. A. 1907. *A Hebrew and English Lexicon of the Old Testament.* Oxford: Clarendon Press.

Buswell, J. O., Jr. 1962. *A Systematic Theology of the Christian Religion.* Grand Rapids: Zondervan.

Charles, R. H., ed. 1913. *Apocrypha and Pseudepigrapha of the Old Testament.* 2 vols. Oxford: Clarendon Press.

Holladay, W. L. 1971. *A Concise Hebrew and Aramaic Lexicon of the Old Testament.* Grand Rapids: Eerdmans.

Kaiser, W. C., ed. 1972. *Classical Evangelical Essays in Old Testament Interpretation.* Grand Rapids: Baker.

Rahlfs, A., ed. 1962. *Septuaginta.* 7th ed. Stuttgart: Württembergische Bibelanstalt.

Other Works

Balmer, E., and Wylie, P. 1962. *When Worlds Collide.* New York: Warner.

Films

Evolution and the Origin of Life. 1973. Del Mar, CA: CRM Educational Films.

Appendix 1

1

Ewing, M., Worzel, J. L., et al., 1969. Shipboard site reports. In *Initial reports of the Deep Sea Drilling Project,* vol. 1, pt. 1, pp. 10-317, *Log 1 of cruises of Glomar Challenger.* Wash., DC: U. S. Govt. Printing Office.

Goodell, H. G. and Garman, R. K., 1969. Carbonate geochemistry of Superior deep test well, Andros Island, Bahamas. *Am. Assoc. Petrol. Geologists Bull.* 53: 513-36.

2

Bathurst, R. G. C., 1971. *Developments in Sedimentology #12, Carbonate Sediments and their Diagenesis.* New York: Elsevier Pub. Co. (Chapter 7, Growth of ooids, pisolites, and grapestone.)

Cloud, P. E., Jr., 1962. Environment of calcium carbonate deposition west of Andros Island, Bahamas. *U. S. Geol. Surv. Profess. Paper,* no. 350.

Donahue, J., 1969. Genesis of oolite and pisolite grains—An energy index. *Jour. Sedimentary Petrology* 39:1399-1411.

Illing, L. V., 1954. Bahamian calcareous sands. *Am. Assoc. Petrol. Geologists Bull.* 38:1-95.

Newell, N. D., Purdy, E. G., and Imbrie, J., 1960. Bahamian oolitic sand. *Jour. Geology,* 68:481-97.

3

Davies, D. K., Ethridge, F. G., and Berh, R. R., 1971. Recognition of barrier environments. *Am. Assoc. Petrol. Geologists Bull.,* 55: 550-65.

Friedman, G. M., 1970. The Bahamas and Southern Florida—A model for carbonate deposition. *Shale Shaker* 21:4-17. (This is an especially helpful article, with a good bibliography. *Shale Shaker* is published by the Oklahoma City Geological Society, Inc., 1020 Cravens Building, Oklahoma City, OK 73102.)

____________, 1969. Depositional environments in carbonate rocks—an introduction. In *Depositional Environments in Carbonate Rocks:* Soc. of Econ. Paleontologists and Mineralogists, Spec. Publ. no. 14, pp. 1-3.

____________, 1971. Petroleum geology—criteria for recognition of depositional environments in carbonate rocks. *McGraw-Hill Encyclopedia of Science and Technology,* 3rd ed. New York: McGraw-Hill Book Co.

Ladd, H. S., ed., 1957. *Treatise on Marine Ecology and Paleoecology, Vol. II., Paleoecology.* Geol. Soc. Amer. Mem. 67.

Lowman, S. W., 1949. Sedimentary facies in Gulf coast. *Am. Assoc. Petrol. Geologists Bull.* 33:1939-97.

Natland, M. L., 1933. The temperature and depth distribution of some recent and fossil Foraminifera in the Southern California region. *Bull. Scripps Inst. Oceanog.* 3:225-30.

Purdy, E. G., 1964. Sediments as substrates. In *Approaches to Paleoecology,* eds. J. Imbrie and N. Newell, pp. 238-71. New York: Wiley.

Stanley, S. M., 1966. Paleoecology and diagenesis of Key Largo limestone, Florida. *Amer. Assoc. Petrol. Geologists Bull.* 50:1927-47.

Walker, K. R., 1972. Community ecology of the Middle Ordovician Black River Group of New York State. *Geol. Soc. Amer. Bull.* 83:2499-2524.

Walton, E. R., 1964. Recent foraminiferal ecology and paleoecology. In *Approaches to Paleoecology,* eds. J. Imbrie and N. Newell, pp. 151-237. New York: Wiley.

4

American Geological Institute, 1973. Across the southern Indian Ocean aboard the Glomar Challenger. *Geotimes* 18: no. 3, pp. 16-19.

Ewing, M., Ewing, J. I., and Talwani, M., 1964. Sediment distribution in the oceans; the Mid-Atlantic Ridge. *Geol. Soc. Amer. Bull.* 75:17-36.

Hays, J. D. and Opdyke, N. D., 1967. Antarctic Radiolaria, magnetic reversals, and climatic change. *Science* 158:1001-11.

Heezen, B. C., et al., 1972. Deep Sea Drilling, Log 20. *Geotimes* 17: no. 4, pp. 10-14.

Keen, M. J., 1968. *An Introduction to Marine Geology.* Elmsford, NY: Pergamon Press. (Chap. 4, Pelagic Sediments.)

Ninkovich, D., Opdyke, N., Heezen, B. C., and Foster, J. H., 1966. Paleomagnetic stratigraphy, rates of deposition and tephrachronology in North Pacific deep-sea sediments. *Earth and Planetary Science Letters* 1:476ff.

Opdyke, N. D., Glass, B., Hays, J. D., and Foster, J., 1966. Paleomagnetic study of Antarctic deep-sea cores. *Science* 154:349-57.

Pessagno, E. A., Jr., 1969. Mesozoic planktonic Foraminifera and Radiolaria. In *Initial Reports of the Deep Sea Drilling Project,* vol. 1, pp. 607-21. *Log 1 of cruises of Glomar Challenger.* Wash., DC: U. S. Govt. Printing Office.

Phillips, J. D., et al., 1967. Paleomagnetic stratigraphy and micropaleontology of three deep sea cores from the central north Atlantic Ocean. *Earth and Planetary Science Letters* 4:118ff.

Riedel, W. R., 1963. The preserved record—Paleontology of pelagic sediments. In *The Sea,* ed. M. N. Hill, vol. 3, pp. 866-87. New York: Interscience.

Rodgers, J., 1957. The distribution of marine carbonate sediments—a review. In *Regional Aspects of Carbonate Deposition, a Symposium, Soc. of Econ. Paleontologists and Mineralogists,* Spec. Pub. no. 5, pp. 1-13.

Weser, O. E., 1970. Lithologic summary. In *Initial Reports of the Deep Sea Drilling Project,* vol. 5, pp. 569-620. *Log 5 of cruises of Glomar Challenger.* Wash., DC: U. S. Govt. Printing Office.

5

Bathurst, R. G. C., 1971. *Developments in Sedimentology #12, Carbonate Sediments and their Diagenesis.* New York: Elsevier Pub. Co. (Several chapters of this work describe processes of burial and chemical change of skeletal remains in coastal environments.)

Behrens, E. E., and Frishman, S. A., 1971. Stable carbon isotopes in blue-green algal mats. *Jour. Geol.* 79:94-100.

Emery, K. O., Tracey, J. I., Jr., and Ladd, H. S., 1954. Bikini and nearby atolls, Marshall Island; Part I, Geology. *U. S. Geol. Surv. Profess. Paper,* no. 260A.

Johnson, J. H., 1961. *Limestone-building Algae and Algal Limestones.* Golden, CO:

Colorado School of Mines.

Kendall, C. G. St. C., and Skipworth, P. A. d'E., 1968. Recent algal mats of a Persian gulf lagoon. *Jour. Sed. Petrology* 38:1040-58.

Scoffin, T. P., 1972. Fossilization of Bermuda patch reefs. *Science* 178:1280-82. (For processes of burial and chemical change of plant and animal remains in sea floor and coral reef environments, also see sections 4 and 12 of this bibliography.)

6

Atwood, D. K., and Bubb, J. N., 1970. Distribution of dolomite in a tidal flat environment, Sugarloaf Key, Florida. *Jour. Geol.* 78:499-505.

Blatt, H. B., Middleton, G., and Murray, R., 1972. *Origin of Sedimentary Rocks.* Englewood Cliffs, NJ: Prentice-Hall.

Chilingar, G. V., Bissell, H. J., and Wolf, K. H., 1967. Diagenesis of carbonate rocks. In *Developments in Sedimentology #8, Diagenesis in Sediments,* eds. G. Larsen and G. V. Chilingar, pp. 179-322. New York: Elsevier Pub. Co. (Pages 287-98 deal with diagenesis of dolomites.)

Friedman, G. M., and Sanders, J. E., 1967. Origin and occurrence of dolostones. In *Developments in Sedimentology #9, Carbonate Rocks,* eds. G. V. Chilingar, H. J. Bissell and R. W. Fairbridge, pp. 267-348. New York: Elsevier Pub. Co.

Ham, W. E., 1951. Dolomite in the Arbuckle Limestone, Arbuckle Mountains, Oklahoma. *Geol. Soc. Am. Bull.* 62:1446-47.

Hayes, P. T., 1964. Geology of the Guadalupe Mountains, New Mexico. *U. S. Geol. Surv. Profess. Paper,* no. 446.

Jodry, R. L., 1969. Growth and dolomitization of Silurian reefs, St. Clair County, Michigan. *Am. Assoc. Petrol. Geologists Bull.* 53:957-81.

Maher, J. C., ed., 1960. Stratigraphic cross section of paleozoic rocks, west Texas to northern Montana. *Am. Assoc. Petrol. Geologists, Cross Section Publication,* no. 2.

Murray, R. C., 1969. Hydrology of South Bonaire, N. A.—A rock selective dolomitization model. *Jour. Sed. Petrology* 39:1007-13.

Shinn, E. A., 1968. Selective dolomitization of recent sedimentary structures. *Jour. Sed. Petrology* 38:612-16.

__________, Ginsburg, R. N., and Lloyd, R. M., 1965. Recent supratidal dolomite from Andros Island, Bahamas. In *Dolomitization and Limestone Diagenesis–A Symposium,* eds. L. C. Pray and R. C. Murray, pp. 112-23. Soc. of Econ. Paleontologists and Mineralogists, Spec. Pub. no. 13.

__________, and Lloyd, R. M., 1969. Anatomy of a modern carbonate tidal flat, Andros Island, Bahamas. *Jour. Sed. Petrology* 39:1202-28.

7

Anderson, R. Y., Dean, W. E., Jr., Kirkland, D. W., and Snider, H. I., 1972. Permian Castile varved evaporite sequence, west Texas and New Mexico. *Geol. Soc. Am. Bull.* 83:59-86.

Dean, W. E., Jr., 1967. *Petrologic and Geochemical Variations in the Permian Castile Varved Anhydrite, Delaware Basin, Texas, and New Mexico.* Ph.D. thesis. University of New Mexico, Albuquerque, NM.

Fuller, J. G. C. M., and Porter, J. W., 1969. Evaporite formations with petroleum reservoirs in Devonian and Mississippian of Alberta, Saskatchewan, and North Dakota. *Am. Assoc. Petrol. Geologists Bull.* 53:909-26. (There are also twelve other articles on evaporites and evaporite deposits in this April, 1969 issue of the *Bulletin*.)

Hsũ, K. J., 1972. When the Mediterranean dried up. *Scientific American*, 227: 27-36.

Kirkland, D. W., and Anderson, R. Y., 1970. Microfolding in the Castile and Todilto evaporites, Texas and New Mexico. *Geol. Soc. Am. Bull.* 81:3259-82.

Ryan, W. B. F., Hsũ, K. J., et al., 1973. *Initial Reports of the Deep Sea Drilling Project*, vol. 13, pt. 1 and pt. 2. Wash., DC: U. S. Govt. Printing Office.

Smith, R., ed., 1967. Stratigraphic cross section of paleozoic rocks, Oklahoma to Saskatchewan. *Am. Assoc. Petrol. Geologists, Cross Section Publication,* no. 5.

8

Dżulyński, S., and Walton, E. K., 1965. *Developments in Sedimentology #7, Sedimentary Features of Flysch and Greywackes.* New York: Elsevier Pub. Co.

Grim, R. E., 1962. *Applied Clay Minerology.* New York: McGraw-Hill Book Co.

Lajoie, J., ed., 1970. Flysch Sedimentology in North America. In *The Geological Assoc. of Canada, Spec. Paper,* no. 7.

Millot, G., 1970. *Geology of Clays; Weathering, Sedimentology, and Geochemistry,* trans. W. R. Farrand and H. Paquet. New York: Springer-Verlag.

9

Edmondson, C. H., 1929. Growth of Hawaiian corals. *Bernice P. Bishop Museum Bulletin,* no. 58. Honolulu, HI.

Emery, K. O., Tracey, J. I., Jr., and Ladd, H. S., 1954. Bikini and nearby atolls, Marshall Island: Part 1, Geology. *U. S. Geol. Surv. Profess. Paper,* no. 260A.

Hoffmeister, J. E., 1964. Growth rate estimates of a Pleistocene coral reef in Florida. *Geol. Soc. Amer. Bull.* 75:353-58.

Ladd, H. S., and Schlanger, S. O., 1960. Bikini and nearby atolls, Marshall Islands, drilling operations on Eniwetok atoll. *U. S. Geol. Surv. Profess. Paper,* no. 260Y.

______________, 1961. Reef-building. *Science* 134:703-15.

Mayor, A. G., 1924. Growth rate of Samoan corals. In *Papers from the Department of Marine Biology of the Carnegie Institute of Washington* 19:51-72. Wash., DC: Carnegie Inst. Pub., no. 340.

10

Barss, D. L., Copland, A. B., and Ritchie, W. D., 1970. Geology of the Middle Devonian reefs, Rainbow area, Alberta, Canada. In *Geology of Giant Petroleum Fields, Am. Assoc. Petrol. Geologists Memoir 14*, ed. M. T. Halbouty, pp. 19-49.

Hriskevich, M. E., 1970. Middle Devonian reef production, Rainbow area, Alberta, Canada. *Am. Assoc. Petrol. Geologists Bull.* 54:2260-81.

Langton, J. R., and Chin, G. E., 1968. Rainbow member facies and related reservoir properties, Rainbow Lake, Alberta. *Am. Assoc. Petrol. Geologists Bull.* 52: 1925-55.

Harbaugh, J. W., 1964. Significance of marine banks in southeastern Kansas in interpreting cyclic Pennsylvanian sediments. *Kansas Geol. Survey Bull.,* no. 169, pp. 199-203.

Heckel, P. H., and Cooke, J. M., 1969. Phylloid algal-mound complexes in outcropping upper Pennsylvanian rocks of mid-continent. *Am. Assoc. Petrol. Geologists Bull.* 53:1058-74.

Johnson, J. H., 1961. *Limestone-building Algae and Algal Limestones.* Golden, CO: Colorado School of Mines.

Klement, Karl W., 1969. Phylloid algal banks (abs.). *Am. Assoc. Petrol. Geologists Bull.* 53:207-08.

Merriam, D. F. and Sneath, P. H. A., 1967. Comparison of cyclic rock sequences, using cross-association. In *Essays in Paleontology and Stratigraphy.* Dept. of Geol., U. of Kansas Spec. Pub. no. 2, pp. 523-38.

Moore, R. C., 1962. Geological understanding of cyclic sedimentation represented by Pennsylvanian and Permian rocks of northern Midcontinent region. In *Geoeconomics of the Pennsylvanian Marine Banks in Southeast Kansas.* Kansas Geol. Soc. 27th Fld. Conf. Guidebook, pp. 91-100.

Myers, D. A., Stafford, P. T., and Burnside, R. J., 1956. Geology of the Late Paleozoic Horseshoe atoll in West Texas. *University of Texas Publication,* no. 5607. Austin, TX: Bureau of Economic Geology.

11

Berry, W. B. N., and Barker, R. M., 1968. Fossil bivalve shells indicate longer month and year in Cretaceous than present. *Nature* 217:938-39.

Mazzullo, S. J., 1971. Length of the year during the Silurian and Devonian Periods—New Values. *Geol. Soc. Amer. Bull.* 82:1085-86.

Runcorn, S. K., 1966. Corals as paleontological clocks. *Scientific American* 215:26-33.

Scrutton, C. T., 1965. Periodicity in Devonian coral growth. *Paleontology* 7:552-58.

12

Achauer, C. W., 1969. Origin of Capitan Formation, Guadalupe Mountains, New Mexico and Texas. *Am. Assoc. Petrol. Geologists Bull.* 53:2314-23. Blatt, H. B., et al. (See section #6 above.)

Duff, P. McL. D., Hallam, A., and Walton, E. K., 1967. *Developments in Sedimentology #10, Cyclic Sedimentation.* New York: Elsevier Pub. Co.

Frost, J. G., 1968. Algal banks of the Dennis Limestone (Pennsylvanian) of eastern Kansas. Unpublished Ph.D. dissertation. Kansas University, Lawrence, KS.

Harbaugh, J. W., 1962. Geologic guide to Pennsylvanian marine banks, southeast Kansas. In *Geoeconomics of the Pennsylvanian Marine Banks in Southeast Kansas.* Kansas Geol. Soc. 27th Fld. Conf. Guidebook, pp. 13-67.

Newell, N. D., et al., 1953. *The Permian Reef Complex of the Guadalupe Mountains Region, Texas and New Mexico.* San Francisco: W. H. Freeman and Co.

Peterson, J. A., and Hite, R. J., 1969. Pennsylvanian evaporite-carbonate cycles and their relation to petroleum occurrence, southern Rocky Mountains. *Am. Assoc. Petrol. Geologists Bull.* 53: 884-908.

Stafford, P. T., 1959. Geology of part of the Horseshoe atoll in Scurry and Kent Counties, Texas. *U. S. Geol. Surv. Profess. Paper,* no. 315A.

Vest, E. L., Jr., 1970. Oil fields of Pennsylvanian-Permian Horseshoe atoll, west Texas. In *Geology of Giant Petroleum Fields, Am. Assoc. Petrol. Geologists Memoir* 14. ed. M. T. Halbouty, pp. 185-203.

Wray, J. L., 1962. Pennsylvanian algal banks, Sacramento Mountains, New Mexico. In *Geoeconomics of the Pennsylvanian Marine Banks in Southeast Kansas.* Kansas Geol. Soc. 27th Fld. Conf. Guidebook, pp. 129-133.

Logan, B. W., Rezak, R., and Ginsburg, R. N., 1964. Classification and environmental significance of algal stromatolites. *Jour. Geol.* 72:68-83.

13

Am. Assoc. Petrol. Geologists, 1960 to 1968. Stratigraphic Cross Section series. (See Maher, J. C., ed., 1960, in section 6 above, and Smith, R., ed., 1967, in section 7 above.)

Goodell, H. G., and Garman, R. K., 1969. (See section 1 above.)

Hughes, P. W., 1954. New Mexico's deepest oil test. In *Guidebook of Southeastern New Mexico (Fifth Field Conference),* pp. 124-130. New Mexico Geol. Soc.

Roswell Geological Society, 1958. North-South Stratigraphic Cross Section, Delaware Basin to Northwest Shelf, Southeastern New Mexico. (A vertical section map of an oil producing area.)

West Texas Geological Society, 1963. Cross Section through Delaware and Val Verde basins from Lea County, New Mexico to Edwards County, Texas. (A vertical section map of an oil producing area.)

14

Information on the structure and density of mollusk and arthropod shells or exoskeletons can be obtained from standard works in paleontology, such as:

Easton, W. H., 1960. *Invertebrate Paleontology.* New York: Harper & Row, Inc.

Shrock, R. R., and Twenhofel, W. H., 1953. *Principles of Invertebrate Paleontology.* New York: McGraw-Hill Book Co.

Information on the specific location of various species in local stratigraphic columns can be obtained from well drilling records, and from works on specific geologic formations and periods in a restricted geographic area. For example, many such sources are listed on pages 154-162 of *Bibliography of Permian Basin Geology, West Texas and Southeastern New Mexico,* West Texas Geological Society, 1967.

Horowitz, A. S., and Potter, P. E., 1971. *Introductory Petrography of Fossils.* New York: Springer-Verlag.

15

Brown, C. W., 1961. Cenozoic stratigraphy and structural geology, northeast Yellowstone National Park, Wyoming and Montana. *Geol. Soc. Amer. Bull.* 72: 1173-94.

Dorf, E., 1960. Tertiary fossil forests of Yellowstone National Park, Wyoming. In *Billings Geological Society Guidebook* (Eleventh Annual Field Conference), pp. 253-60.

———, 1964. The petrified forests of Yellowstone Park. *Scientific American* 210:106-14.

16

Ewing, J., and Ewing, M., 1967. Sediment distribution on the mid-ocean ridges with respect to spreading of the sea floor. *Science* 156:1590-92.

Ewing, M., Ewing, J. I., and Talwani, M., 1964. Sediment distribution in the oceans—the Mid-Atlantic Ridge. *Geol. Soc. Amer. Bull.* 75:17-36.

Gartner, S., Jr., 1970. Sea-floor spreading, carbonate dissolution level, and the nature of Horizon A. *Science* 169:1077-79.

Pitman, W. C., III, and Talwani, M., 1972. Sea-floor spreading in the North Atlantic. *Geol. Soc. Amer. Bull.* 83:619-46.

Vine, F. J., 1966. Spreading of the ocean floor—new evidence. *Science* 154: 1405-15.

17

Burek, P. J., 1970. Magnetic reversals—their applications to stratigraphic problems. *Am. Assoc. Petrol. Geologists Bull.* 54:1120-39.

Cox, A., Dalrymple, G. B., and Doell, R. R., 1967. Reversals of the earth's magnetic field. *Scientific American* 216:44-54.

Dunn, J. R., Fuller, M., Ito, H., and Schmidt, V. A., 1971. Paleomagnetic study of a reversal of the earth's magnetic field. *Science* 172:840-45.

Hays, J. D., and Opdyke, N. D., 1967. Antarctic Radiolaria, magnetic reversals and climatic change. *Science* 158:1001-11.

Foster, J. H., and Opdyke, N. D., 1970. Upper Miocene to Recent magnetic stratigraphy in deep-sea sediments. *Jour. Geophys. Research* 75:4465-73.

Strangway, D. W., 1970. *History of the Earth's Magnetic Field.* New York: McGraw-Hill Book Co.

18

Dalrymple, G. B. and Lanphere, M. A., 1969. *Potassium-Argon Dating.* San Francisco: W. H. Freeman and Co.

———, and Moore, J. G., 1968. Argon 40—excess in submarine pillow basalts from Kilauea volcano, Hawaii. *Science* 161:1132-35.

Indexes

Subject

Biblical References